20 NEW WAYS OF TEACHING THE BIBLE

20 NEW WAYS OF TEACHING THE BIBLE

Donald L. Griggs

A Griggs Educational Resource

published by

Abingdon Press
Nashville

20 New Ways of Teaching the Bible
Copyright © 1977 Griggs Educational Service

Abingdon Edition 1979
Sixth Printing 1983

ISBN 0-687-42740-1

Preface

Ten years ago I began conducting workshops for church teachers throughout Northern California. One of the more popular workshops was "Creative Ways to Teach the Bible." Often after workshops someone would ask, "Where can I get some more ideas like we experienced in the workshop? Do you have any outlines printed that we could use with our students?" Such questions and requests prompted me to write some of my ideas in the form of brief outlines with suggested activities and resources. Eventually I had a collection of twenty outlines of creative approaches to teaching the Bible. I mimeographed the outlines to use and distribute in workshops.

One thing led to another until one day Pat and I found ourselves printing our first book on our own little offset printing machine in our garage. That first book was 20 WAYS OF TEACHING THE BIBLE. Eventually we could no longer spend the time and energy doing our own printing and we took the big step to pay a printer to print our books for us. The first book to be printed commercially was 20 WAYS OF TEACHING THE BIBLE. After seven years, four printings and 14,000 copies we have decided to retire our first book.

However, we continue to receive requests for 20 WAYS OF TEACHING THE BIBLE and now we have developed many more ways to approach teaching the Bible creatively. So, with this book we have prepared outlines for twenty new ways of teaching the Bible. This book continues the basic outline and style of the original book. We have tried to be more complete in our suggestions of what to do with students in the classroom. And, we have tried to consider a wider variety of settings and approaches for specific topics.

As soon as you skim the book you will notice there are more than twenty ways outlined. We have included five or six of the "ways" that were part of the original book that have not been reprinted in any of our other books. Also, in several of the "ways" in this book we have presented more than one approach to the theme. When you add up all the various ways of teaching the Bible that are included there may be as many as forty to fifty different ways to approach teaching the Bible.

Even though this book has my name on it as the author and I developed and used most of these ways myself, I think everyone should know what I can never forget - this book would have never made it to the printer or to you without the suggestions, the critique, the typing, the patience and the love that Pat gave through the past four months when this was the top item on the agenda. I am truly blessed to be able to work, live and grow with Pat in the partnership of a marriage, a business and a life shared together.

As a manuscript is completed it is obvious to the author that many persons are involved in the careful preparation of the book for the eventual reader. In addition to all the work Pat has done I want in this space to acknowledge the important contribution of others. The American Bible Society was very generous in granting permission for us to use the line drawings of Annie Vallatton from the GOOD NEWS BIBLE. Roland W. Tapp, of Omega Books, a good friend and colleague in the do-it-yourself approach to publishing was very helpful in providing counsel and encouragement in the fine points of book publishing. Doug Tinney, a young, creative, competent graphic artist has been exceptionally helpful in doing all the time-consuming, necessary work of layout for type size and style and paste up of typed copy. Without these helpful persons the book would still be just raw material. I appreciate each one's special contribution.

Teaching the Bible is serious business. Sharing the Good News of the new life and faith that is offered to persons through Jesus Christ is a ministry for which every Christian, and especially every Christian teacher is responsible. Our hope that accompanies this book is that teachers will be challenged and helped in their efforts to teach the Bible in creative and life-changing ways.

Don Griggs

Donald L. Griggs

Livermore, California
March 1977

Table of Contents

Introduction

What a presumptuous title, 20 NEW WAYS OF TEACHING THE BIBLE! Twenty ways, is that all? Obviously not! There are hundreds of ways to teach the Bible. There are as many ways as there are teachers, or curricula, or resources. It is not a matter of selecting 20 of the best or newest or easiest. In my teaching during the past several years I have worked at a variety of ways to teach the Bible. Some of the ones that worked for me and the students compose the 20 that are included here.

New ways to teach the Bible? In what sense new? They are not new in the sense of never tried before. They are not especially unique or innovative. Rather, they are new to me and my students. They are the product of my own personal struggle to involve students in effective, memorable ways in their study of the Bible. And, they are new because they have not been published before.

20 NEW WAYS OF TEACHING THE BIBLE is an attempt to provide some outlines of workable approaches to teaching the Bible in church classes with older children, youth and adults. These outlines are samples, suggestions, starting places for teaching the Bible. Each of the twenty, and more, ways of teaching the Bible is special in its own way. However, there are some overarching, general pre-suppositions, guidelines, strategies and resources that are applicable to all the "ways".

Supplementing the Introduction and the Twenty-Five Session Outlines is a Bibliography at the back of the book. This Bibliography is an important part of the book because it presents resources that students and teachers can use in their exploration of the Bible.

Some Affirmations About Teaching and Learning with The Bible

The following affirmations do not include everything important about teaching and learning the Bible, but they do serve as a helpful starting place. These affirmations reflect more of an inductive style of teaching and learning than they do a deductive style. There is a place for teachers doing most of the work in the classroom of presenting information and issues and some of the 20 Ways have elements of presentation by the teacher. However, most of the 20 Ways are examples of an inductive style where the students do most of the work with the teachers serving more as guides, facilitators, resource persons, planners, and enablers.

First Affirmation: *Learning happens when persons act, live, decide and relate in ways that are influenced by the subject matter they have studied.*

Remembering some information about a subject does not equal learning. Remembering equals remembering. Remembering plus interpreting plus expressing visually plus relating to contemporary events plus applying to one's own life all adds up to learning.

Inductive activities add a dimension to the learning process that helps bridge the chasm between information about a subject (Amos, for instance) and the meanings and values of that subject making a difference in one's life today.

There is a difference between someone reciting some information as a result of doing "memory work" and recalling an experience that was memorable. I believe that students need many, many experiences of exploring, deciding, acting and relating that will be memorable in the context of their church education activities.

Second Affirmation: *Learning is a result of persons being actively involved in a dynamic process of interaction between teacher and learner, between learners and other learners, between teachers and learners with resources, and between persons and God.*

The key word, or activity, is interaction. Interaction is more than teachers asking questions and students giving correct answers. Interaction is more than intellectual analysis of a subject with a good discussion. Interaction means sharing feelings, values, choices and dreams as well as sharing information and ideas.

A basic component to inductive activities is interaction. For example: One student may interact with the prophet Amos as he/she takes on the role of Amos and responds to the question of an interviewer. The interviewer could be another student, a parent or a teacher.

Third Affirmation: *Teachers serve best as guides, facilitators or enablers for students in the processes of their learning.*

Teachers are not required to be subject matter experts, but they must be informed about the subject and know where to find additional information. Teachers are not required to figure out everything a student should learn and then just transmit it directly to the student. Rather, teachers will be much more helpful to students as they prepare and lead activities that encourage students to become directly involved in their own explorations.

In an inductive style of teaching teachers assume a variety of responsibilities. They set the stage for learning. They give directions one step at a time. They provide reinforcement and encouragement to the students. They interact with students individually, in small groups, and in larger classes. They ask questions to arouse curiosity and encourage reflection.

Fourth Affirmation: *Basic information about a subject is very important. Of even greater importance are the values, attitudes, and principles that can be applied to a person's life in response to the information.*

A student can quote a lot of verses from Amos and the other prophets regarding justice and talk about the issues of justice and injustice in Amos' day as well as today. However, all the information and talk adds up to very little if there is no application to the person's life that is reflected in the ways he/she lives, works, votes, and relates to others by being just or doing justice.

Inductive activities involve students with more than information. They lead students beyond the facts of a subject and involve them in the substance of a subject with all its relevant feelings, values, principles, attitudes and actions.

Fifth Affirmation: *It is more important to uncover something significant about a subject than it is to cover all the details of that subject.*

Teachers often feel a sense of urgency about covering the whole subject, or covering all the suggested activities for a session. Another way to think of covering something is "to hide it from view, to cover it up." Teachers need to be more concerned about uncovering, about disclosing, revealing something specific that is essential and memorable for that session.

Inductive activities are not a way to get at all the facts and details of a subject. You cannot gain a sense of completion or complete coverage of a subject with inductive activities. But, you can uncover something of great significance to a student or for a group of students.

Sixth Affirmation: *Persons are more motivated and consequently learn more when they are able to make choices about what and how they are going to study.*

Choices are essential to motivation and involvement. A session without any choices for students to make is a dull lesson. Many behavior problems are examples of students making choices. The problem is that teachers did not plan for those choices. There is always more than one way to approach a subject, more than one valuable resource, more than one way to respond creatively. Students can make many choices, big choices and little choices, in the process of every session.

Inductive activities encourage (require) students to make choices. They can choose roles with which to identify, resources to use, ways to answer or respond to questions and issues. They can choose priorities, alternatives, and possibilities.

Seventh Affirmation: There are three important stages or aspects to the learning process: Information, Interpretation and Identification, or Application.

Information is important. In order to set the stage for an inductive activity we need some information. This is especially true when Biblical persons, events, or concepts are the subjects of the activities.

But, we don't stop with just information.

Interpretation of the information is also important. When we respond to questions like. . . . Why did it happen? What does it mean? What do you think was important about? we are guiding persons to think, reflect, interpret. To analyze and interpret what something means is very important.

But, we don't stop with just interpretation.

Identification with a person, an event, a situation personalizes the subject. When persons can put themselves in the place of someone else—or, when persons can see in their own lives similarities to subjects from the Bible, then they are closer to being able to apply the subject to themselves, for the subject to make a difference in their own lives.

An effective inductive teaching activity will include all three of these elements.

Ways to use This Book

In writing this book I do not intend that teachers find here a curriculum to use with their classes. There is neither the depth nor breadth of subject matter to qualify this book to be used as curriculum. However, I think this book could be used well to supplement whatever curriculum a teacher is using. When a subject, passage, theme or approach in this book matches something in the regular curriculum then this would be helpful as a supplement by combining ideas and suggestions found here with what is in the teacher's manual. By looking at the ways in this book as samples, or models, or ways to approach teaching the Bible in general, it is possible for teachers to combine the content of their teacher's manual with the strategy in this book in order to create their own lesson plan. Sometimes a particular lesson or unit of study is weak and the teacher is searching for other resources or approaches for teaching. This book may be helpful in those times.

Teachers who are accustomed to writing their own curriculum will find this book, with resources from other publishers, as well as ourselves, a useful source book for suggestions and ideas. This book must be used with other resources and approaches; it is not complete enough to stand alone as a source for curriculum.

The particular session plans in this book could be used in a wide variety of settings for teaching the Bible in church. Some possibilities are:

— Weekend Retreat for youth or adults.
— Short-term elective class for youth or adults
— Intergenerational classes
— Vacation Church School for older children, youth or adults.
— Sample classes in Teacher Training Event
— Series of sessions for Confirmation class
— Elective study group at summer camp

The people kept quiet
(Isaiah 36.21)

1 *Introducing The Bible*

INTRODUCTION

Many churches present a Bible to the children when they are in the fourth or fifth grade. This is a good time for the children because they are developing reading skills, they are eager to read, they are fascinated with the Bible and they are able to gain skills to use other resources to help them understand the Bible. This section will offer some suggestions of ways to approach the Bible in an introductory way. All the suggestions are not intended to be used in one session. Some of the suggestions can be combined with activities from other sections of this book.

The writing of this book has occurred at an opportune time. In October 1976 a new translation of the Bible was presented by the American Bible Society, the GOOD NEWS BIBLE. This Bible completes the translation process which began in 1966 with the publication of GOOD NEWS FOR MODERN MAN, a translation of the New Testament. The GOOD NEWS BIBLE commends itself as a very suitable Bible to give to children as their first Bible. The GOOD NEWS BIBLE:

- — is an easy to read and reliable translation for readers of all ages.
- — includes several hundred line drawings by Annie Vallotton.
- — has an introduction and outline for each book of the Bible.
- — includes a topical heading for each section of every chapter of the Bible.
- — offers several helps which include a word list, a chronology chart, twelve maps and a subject index.
- — is available direct from the American Bible Society in paperback and hard cover for very few dollars. (See Bibliography for address)

This section will feature the GOOD NEWS BIBLE as an excellent resource for introducing the Bible to children, youth or adults. Many of the suggestions could be adapted and used with other translations.

Activity One/Observations About the Bible

Students work in groups of three to five persons.

Each person needs his/her own Bible to use. It is preferable for everyone to be using the same translation and edition of the Bible.

The teacher can give the following directions:

> Look at the Bible. Flip through the pages. Make a list of the many things you notice about the Bible. Take five minutes to work as a group to write a list of as many observations as you can of what you notice as being special or unique about the Bible. There are no wrong answers.

Someone in each group should record on a piece of paper all the observations of the group.

After five minutes the teacher calls "time" then begins to make a composite list of Bible observations. Write the list on an overhead transparency, chalkboard or sheet of newsprint.

The teacher could summarize by commenting on:

- — How much the class knows about the Bible.
- — How unique and different the Bible is compared to other books.
- — How observant they were.

An excellent resource for students to use after they have browsed through their Bibles is a little pamphlet titled, THE BIBLE AND YOU. This is from the series of pamphlets called Scriptographic Booklets which sell for about 25 to 50 cents each. (See Bibliography for the source).

Activity Two/Questions About the Bible

The class is divided into several small groups of three to five persons.

Each person in a group writes on a slip of paper one or two questions. Or, if the group prefers, one person in the group could write down all the questions stated by the others in the group.

Small groups exchange their sets of questions with each other. Each group reads the new set of questions and selects several questions to share with the whole class.

Make a composite list of questions from all the groups. Record questions so they will be visible for everyone and available at a later time.

The teacher can respond to the list of questions. A few of the questions could be answered directly. However, the teacher's comments may be more appropriate if they include the following:

- All questions are good questions.
- Although we wish that someone might give us all the answers it is important that we work at finding our own answers.
- We need to learn how to use some of the resources within the Bible and some other study tools and to discover which ones will help us with specific questions.
- After we have spent a few weeks exploring the Bible we will return to our questions to see how many we can answer.

Activity Three/The Line Drawings

One of the most helpful and attractive features of the GOOD NEWS BIBLE is the many line drawings created by Annie Vallotton. Annie expresses in just a few simple, yet profound, lines the meaning of an event or the feelings of a person. We could use the line drawings in many ways.

A. Each student search for *one* line drawing that speaks especially to him/her. Read the passage that the drawing accompanies. Then share the passage and the drawing with other students and explain why that drawing was selected.

B. Trace one or more line drawings on an overhead transparency and write a brief story to interpret the drawing.

C. Copy a dozen or more line drawings on a stencil, ditto, or offset master. The teacher could then read one passage at a time and the students can discuss which drawing matches the passage. If there are differences of opinion so much the better; students can compare and discuss the reasons for their choices.

D. Line drawings could form the basis or inspiration for students to create their own line drawings, write their own stories, or make their own collage with line drawings, photos, etc.

Activity Four/The Word List

There are 162 key words from Old and New Testaments that are included in the Word List in the GOOD NEWS BIBLE. Not all words are equally important for any group of students, but there are several ways the Word List could be used.

A. The words could be used to create a crossword puzzle and the brief definitions could serve as the clues for the puzzle.

B. A class could use some words from the List and add to them their own set of important words to develop a glossary or working vocabulary of key biblical concepts.

C. One word could provide the focus for the beginning of a lesson. In addition to the Word List students could use the Index, a Bible dictionary, a Bible concordance and/or a Bible word book to explore further the meanings of the words.

D. Words and definitions could be used to make up word games, matching activities and other fun reinforcing devices.

Activity Five/The Chronology Chart

In three pages all of the major events and persons in the Bible are identified by date in chronological order. This chart will be a handy reference whenever one wants to check the dating of a particular part of the Bible story.

A teacher could select a segment of the chronology chart and guide students to use dictionary and concordance to find key passages that are connected to that particular historical period.

Students will want to use the chronology chart when they do the Bible person time-line in section Five of this book.

Activity Six/The Subject Index

The GOOD NEWS BIBLE is the only Bible I know of that includes a Subject Index. An Index is different from a Concordance. A Concordance cites verses where a particular word appears. For example: under the heading of "Parable" in a Concordance there would be a listing of verses where the word parable appears. The problem for the student who wants to find the parables of Jesus is that not all parables are introduced by, nor do they include, the word parable itself. A subject Index, as in the GOOD NEWS BIBLE, is much more helpful in that it lists all the parables told by Jesus as well as parables told by others. (There are forty-four parables of Jesus listed). The same is true of all the other words in the Index.

There are 349 words included in the Subject Index. Most of the words are names of persons and places. In addition there are many other key words such as love, peace, covenant, etc. Many of the activities in the other sections of this book recommend that the students use the Index from the GOOD NEWS BIBLE. It may be helpful to devise an activity or two that would give the students practice in using the Subject Index.

Let us not give up the habit of meeting together.
(Hebrews 10.25)

Developing Bible Skills* 2

INTRODUCTION

This unit was used with a group of thirty persons. The youngest was six years old. There were about eight elementary and five youth and the rest were adults. There were nine families represented by one or more of their members. The unit was designed for persons with reading skills, so when a six year old child showed up we were surprised. The parents felt that their son would make out fine and would have a good time even though he could not read well. That proved to be true since there were many filmstrips and books with stories and pictures. Also, the six year old was free to participate or not according to how he and his parents decided.

Since this unit depends upon reading skills, older learners were encouraged to team up with younger learners to provide the skills that were necessary to complete the planned activities. Reading aloud, exchanging ideas, asking and answering questions, and searching together for information became the norm for the class. The learners of all ages became "teachers" for each other.

We believe that it is important for students in the church of all ages to develop skills that will help them in studying the Bible. Children receive Bibles in third or fourth grade in many churches. Parents and youth have often either not learned basic Bible Skills or have not practiced them in order to maintain the skills. With this being true of persons in many churches, we think a unit focusing on Bible Skills can be very helpful and also a lot of fun. Our experience has been that all learners with abilities to read and to do some limited research are motivated to participate and receive much satisfaction from activities as outlined below.

This unit was prepared for a week-end family retreat. We had a total of two to four hours for the activities outlined here. To use this unit in a weekly setting of one hour sessions there must be some careful tailoring of the activities to fit the time, space, class, etc.

Step One/Using A Bible Concordance

Sometimes we have questions about where to find particular Bible passages or we want additional passages on a specific subject. A Bible Concordance is a very helpful tool for finding Bible passages.

Each participant, or pair of participants, should have a Concise Bible Concordance in front of him/her.

Show on a chart or transparency the following definition:

"A Concordance is an alphabetical list of the important words in a book with references to the passages in which they occur."

Before using a Concordance instruct participants to find the Lord's Prayer in the Bible. (Many persons are not able to find the Lord's Prayer without some help.)

If persons have had difficulty finding the Lord's Prayer the leader can comment:

— *If we depend just on our memory to find passages in the Bible, we are limited.*

— *If we depend on flipping through the pages to find a passage, we are also limited.*

— *To find something specific we need the help of a person who knows where it is, or we need a "tool" like a Concordance.*

Let's use the Concordance. Turn to the word PRAYER. Notice there are lots of verses listed under that word. But, we will not find the Lord's Prayer because that is a title given to a prayer. We need to look under the words that are a part of the prayer itself. What are some words that might help us?

*This section is reprinted from GENERATIONS LEARNING TOGETHER by Donald and Patricia Griggs. For more than thirty additional session plans on creative ways to teach the Bible you will find the activities in this book to be easily adapted for older children, youth and adult classes.

The participants may suggest words such as: Father, Heaven, Hallowed, Kingdom, Earth, Bread, Temptation, etc. (Using THE RSV HANDY CONCORDANCE from Zondervan, persons would have been able to find a verse from the Lord's Prayer under the words Father, Heaven, Hallowed, Temptation and Trespasses.)

On the right is a re-print of the references listed under the word HEAVEN.

In order to provide opportunity to practice the skill of using the Concordance encourage participants to suggest some verses they recall but do not know where to find in the Bible. After searching for half a dozen verses the skill should be reinforced enough for everyone to feel confident in using a Concordance.

A word of caution: When using a Concise Concordance you will not always find every verse you look for. A Concise Concordance is limited in that it includes only the more familiar passages. However, a Concise Concordance will be sufficient for most students most of the time.

Step Two/Using Bible Cross-Reference Footnotes

Jesus was asked by someone: "Which is the great commandment in the law?" Jesus' answer was, "You shall love the Lord your God with all your heart, and with all your soul, and with all your mind." (Matthew 22:37)

Find this passage in the Gospel of Matthew using a Concordance.

Leader introduces cross-reference footnotes at the bottom of the page. Notice bold print numbers are the verses in Matthew and the light print text following is where this verse appears in other places in the Bible.

Following is part of a page from the Revised Standard Version of the Bible.

HEAVEN — S	
God called the firmament *H*.	Gen 1.8
I will rain bread from *h*	Ex 16.4
I..talked with you from *h*.	20.22
It is not in *h*, that you	Deut 30.12
Behold, *h*..cannot contain thee	1Ki 8.27
should make windows in *h*,	2Ki 7.2
Behold, *h*..cannot contain	2Chr 6.18
I ascend to *h*, thou art there!	Ps 139.8
"How you are fallen from *h*,	Isa 14.12
says the LORD: "*H* is my throne	66.1
till *h* and earth pass away,	Mt 5.18
Pray..Our Father who art in *h*,	6.9
H and earth will pass away,	Mk 13.31
Jesus..was taken up into *h*,	16.19n
H and earth will pass away,	Lk 21.33
a light from *h* flashed about	Acts 9.3
the image of the man of *h*.	1Cor 15.49
caught up to the third *h*—	2Cor 12.2
Christ, who has gone into *h*	1Pet 3.22
and lo, in *h* an open door!	Rev 4.1
great multitude in *h*, crying,	19.1
I saw a new *h* and a new earth;	21.1
The *h* are telling the glory of	Ps 19.1
h are high above the earth,	103.11
thy word is firmly fixed in..*h*.	119.89
the *h* languish..with the earth.	Isa 24.4
the *h* above..withheld dew,	Hag 1.10
he saw the *h* opened and the	Mk 1.10
powers of the *h*..be shaken.	Lk 21.26
by the word of God *h* existed	2Pet 3.5
we wait for new *h* and a new	3.13

MATTHEW 22   24   *The Great Commandment*

living." ³³And when the crowd heard it, they were astonished at his teaching. 34 But when the Pharisees heard that he had silenced the Sad'dū·ceēs̄, they came together. ³⁵And one of them, a lawyer, asked him a question, to test him. ³⁶ "Teacher, which is the great commandment in the law?" ³⁷And he said to him, "You shall love the Lord your God with all your heart, and with all your soul, and with all your mind. ³⁸ This is the great and first commandment. ³⁹And a second is like it, You shall love your neighbor as yourself. ⁴⁰ On these two commandments depend all the law and the prophets."

41 Now while the Pharisees were gathered together, Jesus asked them a question, ⁴² saying, "What do you think of the Christ? Whose son is he?" They said to him, "The son of David." ⁴³ He said to them, "How is it then

and being called rabbi by men. ⁸ But you are not to be called rabbi, for you have one teacher, and you are all brethren. ⁹And call no man your father on earth, for you have one Father, who is in heaven. ¹⁰ Neither be called masters, for you have one master, the Christ. ¹¹ He who is greatest among you shall be your servant; ¹² whoever exalts himself will be humbled, and whoever humbles himself will be exalted.

13 "But woe to you, scribes and Pharisees, hypocrites! because you shut the kingdom of heaven against men; for you neither enter yourselves, nor allow those who would enter to go in.ᵛ ¹⁵ Woe to you, scribes and Pharisees, hypocrites! for you traverse sea and land to make a single proselyte, and when he becomes a proselyte, you make him twice as much a child of h... yourselves.

t Or David in the Spirit   u Other ancient authorities omit hard to bear
v Other authorities add here (or after verse 12) verse 14, Woe to you, scribes and Pharisees, hypocrites! for you devour widows' houses and for a pretense you make long prayers; therefore you will receive the greater condemnation   w Greek Gehenna

22.33: Mt 7.28.   22.34-40: Mk 12.28-34; Lk 20.39-40; 10.25-28.   22.35: Lk 7.30; 11.45; 14.3.
22.37: Deut 6.5.   22.39: Lev 19.18; Mt 19.19; Gal 5.14; Rom 13.9; Jas 2.8.
22.41-46: Mk 12.35-37; Lk 20.41-44.   22.44: Ps 110.1; Acts 2.34-35; Heb 1.13; 10.13.
22.46: Mk 12.34; Lk 20.40.   23.4: Lk 11.46; Acts 15.10.
23.5: Mt 6.1, 5, 16; Ex 13.9; Deut 6.8; Mt 9.20.   23.6-7: Mk 12.38-39; Lk 20.46; 14.7-11; **11.43.**
23.8: Jas 3.1.   23.11: Mt 20.26; Mk 9.35; 10.43; Lk 9.48; 22.26.
23.12: Lk 14.11; 18.14; Mt 18.4, 1 Pet 5.6.   23.13: Lk 11.52.   23.15: Acts 2.10; 6.5; 13.43.
23.16-22: Mt 5.33-37; 15.14.   23.17: Ex 30.29.   23.21: 1 Kings 8.13; Ps 26.8.
23.23-24: Lk 11.42; Lev 27.30; Mic 6.8.

Using the footnotes find the Matthew 22:37 verse in the book of Deuteronomy. Then find it in Mark and Luke. Also, find Matthew 22:39 in Leviticus and other places in the New Testament.

Matthew 22:34-40   Mark 12:28-34   Luke 10:25-28

Spend a few minutes comparing the same passage in Matthew, Mark, and Luke by answering the following questions:

a. Who asks Jesus the questions?
b. Why is Jesus asked the question?
c. What is Jesus' response to the question?
d. How does the questioner respond to Jesus?
e. What else happened?

Notice that there are some differences between the three gospels in terms of some of the details. However, the truth of the message is the same.

Step Three/Using A Bible Dictionary

Each participant, or pair of participants, should have a copy of a Bible Dictionary to use for the following activities. See Bibliography for suggestions of some helpful Bible Dictionaries.

The Bible Dictionary gives more than definitions. Look at the word COVENANT. The paragraph or two includes a description of how the word is used in the Bible, plus some biblical references.

Use the Bible Dictionary to find answers to some of the following questions. Each person, or pair of persons, can choose which questions to answer. Work on as many questions as interest you or as you have time for in the ten minutes we have to work.

SOME QUESTIONS*

a. What is the difference between the two words APOSTLE and DISCIPLE?
b. What is the other name for MT. SINAI? Where is the mountain located?
c. Who was EUTYCHUS? Why was he remembered?
d. What does the name EZEKIEL mean?
e. Who were the SADDUCEES and the PHARISEES?
f. What is a PARABLE?
g. What does the word GOSPEL mean?

---

*These questions are just examples of the types of questions that could be asked. The leader should prepare his/her own list of questions.

After spending ten minutes searching for answers to the questions, persons can share what they have discovered and also share their feelings about the experiences of using Bible Concordances, Footnotes and Dictionaries.

Step Four/Bible Scavenger Hunt

Now that participants in the class have become familiar with some of the basic tools for Bible study it is possible to reinforce those skills and have some fun by playing a Bible Scavenger Hunt.

The leader may desire to reorganize the participants into different groupings. Each group should include five persons. One way to achieve this would be to select the six youngest persons in the class (assuming a class of thirty persons).

Each of these "youngest children" select an older "brother" or "sister". The older "brother" or "sister" choose a "mother" or "father" for their group. The "mother" or "father" chooses another member of the "family."

The "temporary families" will work together on the scavenger hunt. This regrouping gives persons a chance to work with others than those in their own personal family.

Allow twenty minutes for the Scavenger Hunt. Give each participant a worksheet which lists all the items. The leader may want to change, add, or substitute items with those on the worksheet. Use any or all of the tools available for finding information.

After spending twenty minutes searching, announce that "time is up." Check to see which group has the most right answers. Compare all the answers. Be sure each person ends up with a worksheet filled out with the right answers. Spend some time discussing any questions that arise.

Bible Scavenger Hunt

1. Find Deuteronomy 6:5. List three places in the New Testament where this verse is quoted.

   _____ _____ _____

2. Find the shortest _____ and the longest _____ psalms.

3. Find two places in the Old Testament where the Ten Commandments are listed. . .

   _____ _____

4. Name a book in the Bible which represents each of the following kinds of writing.

   Law _____   Prophecy _____
   Poetry _____   Gospel _____
   History _____   Letter _____

4. List the names of all twelve disciples (apostles).

   _____ _____ _____ _____
   _____ _____ _____ _____
   _____ _____ _____ _____

6. Write ten important facts about any person in the Bible.

   _____   _____
   _____   _____
   _____   _____
   _____   _____
   _____   _____

7. State the original occupations of the following Bible persons:

   Moses _____   Jesus _____
   Amos _____   Matthew _____
   Peter _____   Paul _____

8. Determine the approximate mileage between:

   Ur and Haran _____ miles

   Haran and Bethel _____ miles

   Land of Goshen and Mt. Sinai _____ miles

   Nazareth and Bethlehem _____ miles

   Jerusalem and Corinth _____ miles

9. Name six bodies of water mentioned in the Bible

   _____ _____ _____
   _____ _____ _____

10. Place the following events in chronological order:

    _____ Baptism of Jesus   _____ David Anointed King of Israel
    _____ Call of Abraham   _____ Captivity in Babylon
    _____ Preaching of Jeremiah   _____ Day of Pentecost
    _____ Resurrection of Jesus   _____ Creation
    _____ Execution of John the Baptist _____ Feeding of the 5000
    _____ Writing of Gospel of Mark   _____ Captivity in Egypt
    _____ Call of Moses   _____ Paul in Rome

Answers for the Scavenger Hunt:

1. Matt. 22:37, Mark 12:30, Luke 10:27

2. Psalms 117 and 119

3. Exodus 20:1-17 and Deut. 5:6-21

4. Law: Numbers and others
   Poetry: Psalms and others
   History: Acts and others
   Prophecy: Isaiah and others
   Gospel: Matthew, Mark, Luke and John
   Letter: Romans and others

5. Peter, Andrew, James the Son of Zebedee, John, Philip, Bartholomew, Thomas, Matthew (or Levi), James Son of Alphaeus, Thaddaeus, Simon the Cananaan, and Judas Iscariot (from Matthew 10:2-4)

6. Check the list of facts with a Bible Dictionary or other resource.

7. Moses: Sheepherder
   Amos: Sheepherder and dresser of Sycamore trees
   Peter: Fisherman
   Jesus: Carpenter
   Matthew: Tax Collector
   Paul: Tentmaker

8. Use mileage scale on a map in the atlas to determine your estimates

9. Possible correct answers (and there are others)

Dead Sea	Sea of Galilee	Euphrates River
Jordan River	Red Sea	The Great Sea
Sea of Reeds	Mediterranean Sea	
Nile River	Tigris River	

10. Creation, Call of Abraham, Captivity in Egypt, Call of Moses, David anointed King, Preaching of Jeremiah, Captivity in Babylon, Baptism of Jesus, Execution of John the Baptist, Feeding of 5000, Resurrection of Jesus, Day of Pentecost, Paul in Rome, Writing of Gospel of Mark.

So the people of Judah were carried away. (Jeremiah 52.27)

3 An Opinionnaire

INTRODUCTION

Persons have opinions about many subjects, including biblical subjects. Opinions are often the basis on which discussions are conducted. Learning involves more than sharing opinions. It is important to help students to move beyond their opinions, to search deeply into a subject, to challenge the opinions of others, and to clarify and reformulate their own ideas and values.

An opinionnaire is not designed to test knowledge, but rather to stimulate discussion. An opinionnaire is best used at the beginning of a unit of study to help students focus on the subject and to express some of their own ideas and feelings. Teachers can devise opinionnaires with six to a dozen statements that focus on the subject of the particular session.

Since the statements of an opinionnaire are really "loaded" with ambiguity they are intended to provoke differences of opinion rather than elicit a consensus of agreement. If everyone in the class has the same opinion there is not as much potential for discussion as there would be if there are differences of opinion. Many statements are true **and** false depending upon the emphasis a person places on one part of the statement or another part.

After all students have marked their copies of the opinionnaire, time can be spent comparing responses then discussing the reasons for their various points of view. When it becomes clear that there is need for information and other interpretations against which to test their opinions, the students could work individually, in small groups, or as a whole class exploring, reading, interviewing and investigating.

An opinionnaire is a discussion starter and a way to launch a subject; it is not a way to summarize or conclude a subject.

Two sample opinionnaires are presented below. These are intended to be samples. It is important for the teacher to devise his/her own opinionnaires appropriate to a specific class and subject of study.

Opinionnaire #1/The Bible

Check whether you agree or disagree with the following statements.

	Agree	Disagree
1. The first Bible was dictated by God and therefore has no mistakes or contradictions.	_____	_____
2. A person can find most of the answers for life's mysteries and problems by reading the Bible.	_____	_____
3. Some verses in the Bible are more important than other verses.	_____	_____
4. The Old Testament is not a very important document for Christians.	_____	_____
5. The Bible is no more important or special than any other great book.	_____	_____
6. If we read the Bible we will be good persons and God will be pleased with us.	_____	_____
7. The stories and events in the Bible happened so long ago that they don't make any sense or have any meaning to us today.	_____	_____

8. Nobody reads the Bible much any more. _____ _____

9. Scholars should add some new books to the Bible that are more contemporary and relevant. _____ _____

10. The most reliable translation of the Bible is the Revised Standard Version. _____ _____

11. Persons who wrote the Bible included a lot of their own ideas and feelings about God and man. _____ _____

12. The best way to read the Bible is to start with Genesis 1:1 and read all the way through to Revelation. _____ _____

"Teach them to your children."
(Deuteronomy 11:19)

Opinionnaire #2/Jesus

Check whether yo agree or disagree with the following statements.

	Agree	Disagree
1. Jesus is the son of God **because** he was "conceived by the Holy Ghost, born of the virgin Mary."	_____	_____
2. Jesus could have selected some other persons to be his Apostles.	_____	_____
3. Jesus should have explained more directly that he was the Messiah.	_____	_____
4. God should not have allowed Jesus to be killed so early in his life.	_____	_____
5. His resurrection from the dead is the single most important thing about Jesus.	_____	_____
6. If we could pattern our lives after Jesus then we would never have any problems.	_____	_____
7. Jesus will return to the world again, someday.	_____	_____

Whoever believes that Jesus
is the Messiah is a child
of God. (I John 5.1)

4 *Researching A Bible Passage*

INTRODUCTION

There are several ways of reading and studying the Scriptures:

1. Reading familiar passages for inspiration.
2. Reading whole books in order to grasp the overall message or purpose of that book.
3. Doing a word study or topical study by using Bible Concordance and Dictionary to investigate many dimensions and meanings of a specific word or topic.
4. Taking a key chapter or sequence of verses and through use of a variety of resource tools research that passage carefully by working on key words, concepts, references to geography, persons, time, etc.

What follows is a suggested approach to one specific passage of Scripture, Romans 1:1-17. In the right hand margin are representative questions which can be asked concerning these seventeen verses. Persons can answer these questions through use of Bible Commentary, Dictionary, Atlas, Wordbook and Concordance. A teacher or student could take any significant passage, make his/her own list of questions and research the passage in this same manner. This study lends itself to individual or small group work.

Worksheet

(1) Paul, a **servant** of Jesus Christ, called to be an **apostle,** set apart for the **gospel** of God (2) which he promised beforehand through his prophets in the **holy scriptures,** (3) the gospel concerning his Son, who was descended from **David** according to the flesh (4) and designated **Son of God** in power according to the **Spirit** of holiness by his **resurrection** from the dead, Jesus Christ our Lord, (5) through whom we have received **grace** and apostleship to bring about obedience to the faith for the sake of his name among **all nations,** (6) including **yourselves** who are called to belong to Jesus Christ; (7) To all God's beloved in **Rome** who are called to be **saints:**
Grace to you and peace from God our Father and the Lord Jesus Christ. (8) First, I thank my God **through Jesus Christ** for all of you, because your faith is proclaimed in all the world. (9) For God is my witness, whom I serve with my spirit in the gospel of his Son, that without

— see footnote on word **servant**
— check meaning of **apostle**
— see other ref. to **gospel** in vs. 16.

— what are the specific scriptural references?
— what is important about **David?**

— what is the meaning of **Son of God?**
— what is the meaning of **Spirit?**
— why is **Resurrection** important?

— what is the meaning of **grace?**

— why refer to **all nations?**
— who is meant by **yourselves?**

— what is importance of **Rome?**
— check meaning of **saints**
— why such a long greeting vs 1-7?

— why offer prayer **through Jesus Christ?**

ceasing I mention you always in my **prayers,** (10), asking that somehow by God's will I may at last succeed in coming to you. (11) For I long to see you, that I may impart to you some spiritual gift to strengthen you, (12) that is, that we may be mutually encouraged by each other's faith, both yours and mine. (13) I want you to know brethren, that I have often intended to come to you (But thus far have been prevented), in order that I may reap some harvest among you as well as among the rest of the Gentiles. (14) I am under obligation both to **Greeks** and to **Barbarians,** both to the wise and to the foolish; (15) so I am eager to preach the gospel to you also who are in Rome. (16) for I am not ashamed of the **gospel:** it is the power of God for salvation to everyone who has **faith** to the Jew first and also to the Greek. (17) For in it the **righteousness** of God is revealed through faith for faith; **as it is written,** "He who through faith is righteous shall live."

— what is the place of **prayer** in Paul's ministry?
— where was Paul when he wrote the letter?
— the purpose for Paul's planned visit?

— why did Paul write this letter?

— what would have kept Paul from going to Rome?

— what obligation does Paul have?
— who are the **Greeks?**
— who are the **Barbarians?**

— what is the **gospel?**

— what is the meaning of **faith?**
— why to the **Jew first?**
— what is meaning of **righteousness?**

— where is it **written?**

"God bless him who comes in the name of the Lord!" (Matthew 21.9)

5 Overview of Bible Persons in 60 Minutes

INTRODUCTION

This plan could be used at the beginning of a unit of study on the Bible to introduce many of the persons and events of the Bible. Or, it could be used as a review after the class has engaged in a study of the overall scope and drama of the Bible.

Preparation

The teacher needs to prepare several things:

1. On as many pieces of paper as there will be students the teacher writes the name of one key person. Write a different name on each sheet in a corner of the page. (This will work well for as few as 12 and as many as 30 students.) You could make name tags for the students with the names of their Bible persons.

2. Bring to class or otherwise provide a sufficient number of Atlases, Bible Dictionaries, Encyclopedia, or other resource books which are easily read and in which material can be found without difficulty. (See Bibliography for recommended books).

3. Provide enough tables to that students are not too crowded and have adequate work space.

Step One

Announce that today in one hour the class is going to gain an overview of persons and events in the Bible. Each student can select a sheet of paper with the name of a person that he is to study.

Provide the following directions:

Each of you has the name of a different Bible person.

There are a variety of resource books available. Use the Resource books to find as many answers as you can to the following questions:

  a. If the person's name has a special meaning, what is that meaning?
  b. Approximately when did the person live?
  c. What are some important actions or beliefs of the person?
  d. Who are some other persons who were important in your person's life?

Note to the teacher: You may want to mimeograph the above questions on a worksheet that students can use to write their answers. The questions should be visible in some way.

After the students have found some answers to the questions, they can spend a few minutes searching for one or two important Bible passages related to the person.

Step Two

Allow sufficient time for working. Twenty to thirty minutes should be enough. When you sense that everyone has found something then go to the next step. The teacher should circulate among the class to help some who are having difficulty, but try to leave the students free to do their own work.

Step Three

When the teacher feels that all students have sufficient information the following instructions are given:

Put yourself in the place of your person and pretend that you are to introduce yourself to a stranger. Write down two or three sentences to introduce yourself. Write in the first-person. "My name is . . . . . . .and I am remembered because. . . . ."

Allow about five minutes for this task.

Be sure the students keep it brief. By writing these short introductions the students are enabled to summarize their findings and at the same time to identify personally with the person or event they worked on. Also, by writing down a sentence or two each student has something to read in the next step so that no one will be embarrassed by not remembering what to say.

"The Lord anoints you as a ruler of his people."
(I Samuel 10.1)

Step Four

This is the fun step. Tell the students to arrange themselves in chronological order. Leave the class alone. Let them work out the order for themselves. Do not rearrange the order that they finally settle on. Have the class actually stand, or sit, in a large, shallow semicircle. Then begin with the first person by having him introduce himself in the role of his person. When you come to a person out of order ask questions and offer some clues which might help that person or others see their misplacement. Then change the order.

Step Five

If there is time, have the class shuffle all the papers so that each ends up with a different one. Then go through the process of arranging themselves in order again. Also, the papers could be mounted on the wall in chronological order as a reminder during the succeeding weeks of study.

Follow-up Study

Some key questions to ask after the time-line has been introduced are:

a. How do you feel about this "family" of yours?
b. What impressions do you have about these persons and events as a whole?
c. Are there any similarities you recognized among all of the persons?
d. What additional information would you like to have?

In addition to a brief discussion, it would be possible to use this introductory study as the basis for some creative activities that would focus on the Bible persons. Each student in the class could do one of the following activities, or all the students could do the same activity. After the students have expressed their ideas and impressions creatively it is important for them to have time to share their creativity with others in the class. Some possible activities are:

    a. Create one or more write-on slides to illustrate the Bible person(s).
    b. Write a letter **to** or write a letter **from** the Bible person(s).
    c. Develop a pantomime or skit to present some key aspects of the Bible person(s).
    d. Select teaching pictures and write captions to illustrate and interpret the Bible person(s).

Suggested Bible Persons

Abraham	Solomon	John
Isaac	Amos	Andrew
Jacob	Hosea	Mary
Aaron	Timothy	Micah
Ezra	Nehemiah	Saul
Jesus	Deborah	Peter
Rebecca	Judas	Titus
Joseph	Jeremiah	Miriam
Paul	Moses	Ezekiel
Isaiah	Barnabas	Gideon
King Josiah	Joshua	David
Samson	Samuel	Mary Magdalene
John the Baptist	Jonathan	And others chosen
Matthew	Nicodemus	by the teacher.

David tore his clothes in sorrow.
(2 Samuel 1.11)

Comparing the Creation 6 Stories

INTRODUCTION

There are several sources (authors, cultures, traditions) which have contributed to the final product of what we now have in the Scriptures. One very good example of this is the Genesis accounts of Creation in chapters one and two. A teacher should consult one or more of the following resources before using this lesson plan.

1. *Interpreters' Bible*, Vol. 1
2. *Understanding the Old Testament*, Bernard Anderson
3. *Harper's Bible Dictionary*, article on creation

Objectives

At the end of the session students should be able to:

1. State the differences between the two stories of creation in Genesis 1 and 2.
2. Explain why two creation stories are in Genesis.
3. Express in some creative form their own ideas and feelings about the beginnings of the universe and humankind.

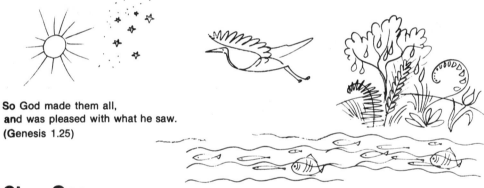

So God made them all,
and was pleased with what he saw.
(Genesis 1.25)

Step One

Divide the class into two smaller groups. Give each person in the group a copy of the worksheet. Appoint one person to be chairman of the group and report the group's answers. Assign each group one of the passages, Genesis 1:1-2:3 or 2:4-25. Remind the students that they are to get their answers **only** from the passage they were assigned.

Step Two

Allow each group to work for 10-15 minutes. Have one person in each group read the passage while the rest follow in their Bibles. After reading, then go back to answer the questions on the basis of the information in their account of creation. While the groups are working, the teacher should be copying the worksheet on a chalk board, on a large sheet of newsprint, or on an overhead transparency.

Step Three

Have both groups report their answers to one question at a time. Record their responses on a large chart. After all the questions are answered, ask the question: "What observations would you make after seeing these two lists of answers?" One fifth grader responded: "It looks like two different guys wrote two different stories and somebody else put them together." That is the point.

Step Four

With the above steps the class could go in one or more of several directions:

1. Participate in a discussion which explores further the differences between the two stories.
2. See a filmstrip that presents the theme of creation.
3. Do some research in the public or school library to try to find other stories of creation.
4. Read or listen to the poem "Creation" from James Weldon Johnson's collection of poems in GOD'S TROMBONES.
5. Search for other passages in the Old Testament that focus on creation and compare these passages with the Genesis passages.

Step Five

The subject of creation lends itself very well to creative expression through art. Several media are possible:

1. Tempra paint using brushes, pieces of sponge, string, toothbrushes.
2. Poetry
3. Tissue paper collage
4. Collage with varieties of natural and "junk" materials.
5. Clay

This creative expression would give the students the opportunity to portray their own personal feelings and responses to the whole theme of creation.

Sample Worksheet

GENESIS 1:1-2:3	QUESTIONS TO ANSWER	GENESIS 2:4-25
1.	How long did creation take?	1.
2.	Where did creation take place?	2.
3.	When in the process was man created?	3.
4.	When in the process was woman created?	4.
5.	From what substance is man and woman created?	5.
6.	What is the relationship between male and female?	6.
7.	What is the relationship between man and God?	7.
8.	What is the main point, idea, or message of the story?	8.

INTRODUCTION

In teaching this session it is important for teachers to have "rehearsed" in their minds all of the procedures of the session. There are a variety of teaching activities and resources recommended. The pace of the session moves quickly and the teacher needs to be prepared for spontaneous responses, questions, and suggestions which may arise from the students.

This particular plan works well with mixed age groups; younger and older children or adults and children. It is also an excellent design for involving teachers in learning through several senses, using a variety of resources and illustrating the inductive approach.

Objectives

At the end of the session the students should be able to:

1. State their understanding of the Psalmist's concept of God and his meaning of the word "hand" in Psalm 95.
2. See and feel the importance, power, and creativity of their own hands.
3. Express creatively their individual responses to Psalm 95:1-7 and the poem "Creation" in James Weldon Johnson's book GOD'S TROMBONES.

Room Arrangement and Teacher Preparation

It would be helpful to divide the room into two parts. For the Biblical study, discussion and listening, place the chairs in a circle. Provide one Bible per chair. Place a screen or bulletin board so that it can be seen by everyone. Also, place the recorder or phonograph so that it can be reached easily by the teacher and heard by the whole class. In the other part of the room (either around the perimeter of the circle or in the other half of the room) have tables (one for each six persons) covered with newspaper or butcher paper. It is best to have chunks of clay already available at the places around the table. Also, provide a dishpan of water and paper towels. It is much more satisfactory to use moist potter's clay available in red, grey, or tan from most art supply stores. Plan for about one pound per student.

Step One

Plan for the students to discuss in pairs the following assignment.

> "Everybody has some 'used-to-thinks.' 'Used-to thinks' are those things you used to think and now don't think any more. We are going to discuss some of our 'used-to-thinks' about God. Share with each other some of the things you used to think about God and don't think in the same way any more."

Allow about five minutes for this.

"I will praise you LORD. . . ."
(Psalms 9.1)

Step Two

Then have the class work in groups of four to six persons to do the following:

   a. Read Psalm 95:1-7.
   b. Discuss two questions:
      1. What do you think is the writer's idea, image, or concept of God? What does he think God is like?
      2. What are some ideas you have about the significance or meaning of the words "hand" and "hands" in this Psalm?

Allow five to eight minutes for this, then provide opportunity for the small groups to share with the whole class some of their ideas.

Psalm 95

O come, let us sing to the Lord;
   let us make a joyful noise to the rock of our salvation!
Let us come into his presence with thanksgiving;
   let us make a joyful noise to him with songs of praise!
For the Lord is a great God,
   and a great King above all gods.
In his hand are the depths of the earth;
   the heights of the mountains are his also.
The sea is his, for he made it;
   for his hands formed the dry land.

O come, let us worship and bow down,
   let us kneel before the Lord, our Maker!
For he is our God,
   and we are the people of his pasture,
   and the sheep of his hand.

(From the RSV Bible)

Step Three

Focus on HANDS. There are many ways to do this. The teacher's own creativity, available resources, and time will determine what is possible.

Some suggestions are: (Don't try to do them all. Try your own approach.)

   A. Have each person look at his/her own hands then respond spontaneously as a group to the following questions:

      1. What are some things that are important or fun that you do with your hands?
      2. What would it be like to be without hands?
      3. Why do you think the Psalmist used the word "hands"?

   B. Do some non-verbal creative expression with hands by encouraging persons to communicate feelings of the following: (Each student could face a partner to be specific in his/her communicating.)

      1. Show anger or frustration.
      2. Show sadness or loneliness.
      3. Express friendship to another person.
      4. Communicate happiness or joy with hands.
      5. Show you need someone else's help.
      6. Play a game with another person using hands.
      7. Shake hands with several people showing them you are glad to see them.

C. Look through magazines to find pictures of hands expressing feelings and actions of hands. Make individual or group montages.

D. Mount several significant pictures or photographs of hands on the tack-board to use as illustrations of feelings. Discuss together what is communicated through these visual expressions.

E. Use a print of the Michelangelo's painting "Creation of Adam" showing creation of man where the hands of God and man are outstretched toward each other. Prepare ahead of time a mask to cover over the whole painting except for a small square which reveals both hands. Discuss the painting.

Step Four

Guide the group to stand in a circle holding hands.

The teacher could ask for students to respond how they feel as a group now, in a circle holding hands, compared to when they first came into the room. Or, the teacher could express some of his/her own feelings then ask for some responses.

After a minute or two ask if anyone thought of the song "He's Got the Whole World in His Hands." Sing the song encouraging students to suggest words to create new verses to the song. Suggest clapping hands to keep the rhythm.

With the group in a circle holding hands or possibly putting hands and arms around each other's shoulders or waists, the feeling of closeness is communicated. Our hands bring us closer to each other. This then would be a natural time for prayer to express thanksgiving for hands and commitment to use our hands for continuing God's creation.

Step Five

Encourage group to sit down. Allow a minute or two for brief, spontaneous conversation in small or larger groups.

Then describe what is to follow:

1. Listen to a poem
2. Go to the table where there is clay.
3. Play and create with the clay in any way that expresses your feelings in response to what we have done or to the poem you will hear.

(These instructions are helpful so as to avoid having to give any instructions between the hearing of the poem and the moving to work with the clay. Instructions at that point are an interruption of the thinking, creating process.)

Read or play the recording of the creation poem in GOD'S TROMBONES.* Encourage the students to listen for all the times when hands or arms are mentioned and what actions they perform.

Step Six

Everyone spends 15-25 minutes creating and playing with the clay. Teachers could participate also. Conversation will most likely be informal.

After time for creating, persons can circulate to see what others have done.

The teacher may want to wrap-up the session by asking the students to reflect upon the day's experience. "How did it feel to use hands to communicate and create?" "What was learned about Psalm 95?"

*GOD'S TROMBONES is available in printed form from a bookstore. James Weldon Johnson is the author, Viking Press the publisher.

*GOD'S TROMBONES, The Poem on Creation, is available in recorded form from: Decca Records, a recording by Fred Waring and his Pennsylvanians.

8 Exodus

INTRODUCTION

There are several ways to study the concept of Exodus. One way would be to focus on the specific *event* of the crossing of the sea and the circumstances that immediately preceded and followed the event. This study would center on the book of Exodus, chapters twelve to fifteen.

Another way to study Exodus would be to study the whole *book* that bears the name. A study of the book of Exodus would deal with many events, many years, and many persons. The study would encompass the whole movement from Egypt to the Promised Land.

In this session we are going to study the *theme* of Exodus as it appears in many books of the Bible. The experience of the Exodus was for the people of Israel the central act of God in all their history for their redemption. In future generations of poets, prophets, priests, and rabbis there would be many references to the action of God in the Exodus. Even in the New Testament, in the writings of the church fathers and more recently in sermons of persons like Martin Luther King, Jr. there are repeated references to the fact and the significance of Exodus.

The activities in which the students will participate in this session will provide the opportunity to explore, discover and interpret the meaning of Exodus in the Bible and in contemporary history.

The activities in this session may take more than one hour.

The Lord made a road through the sea.
(Isaiah 43.16)

Step One/Introduce Exodus

The teacher can introduce the concept of Exodus by making a very brief presentation which would include the following:
   a. Reading a definition from a standard dictionary.
   b. Reading a statement from a Bible dictionary.
   c. Referring to the book of Exodus.
   d. Mentioning the event of the Exodus.
   e. Suggesting that the theme of Exodus permeates the Old and New Testaments.

Step Two/Three Key Bible Passages

Students could work in twos or threes to read the following three passages of Scripture and respond to four questions that are presented below.

The three key Bible passages are:
   a. I Samuel 12:8
   b. Deuteronomy 26:5-9
   c. Joshua 24:2-13

Four key questions related to each passage are:

    a. How, or by what name(s) are the people of God identified?
    b. What actions are directed *against* the people?
    c. What are the actions or reactions *of* the people?
    d. What are Yahweh's actions?

NOTE: Essentially the same message is presented in each of the three passages. We are going to look for other passages in the Old and New Testaments that contain a similar message.

After exploring the three key passages and responding to the four questions, it is important to spend a few minutes comparing notes so that all the students will be able to share their conclusions regarding the theme of Exodus as represented in these three passages.

Step Three/Search For Other Bible Passages

Using Bible Concordances, Dictionaries and other resources encourage students to search for other passages of Scripture in the Old and New Testaments that focus on the theme of Exodus. In using a concordance one would not look for references to the word Exodus. That word does not appear as such. Check words such as Egypt, sea, desert, wilderness, Moses, deliverance, etc.

Some sample passages include:

    Psalms 78, 105, and 106.
    Isaiah 40:3-5, 41:17-20, 43:1-3 and 43:14-19
    Hosea 11:1-4, 12:9,13 and 13:1-3
    Jeremiah 31:31-37 and 33:14-26
    Acts 13:16-19
    I Corinthians 10:1-6

As the students find one or two passages (or the teacher could suggest passages if they have a hard time finding anything) they could apply the above four questions to each passage to see whether or not the same four emphases are present. Chances are that at least two or three of the four emphases will be found.

Step Four/Exodus Today

There are several resources that could be used to search for the presence of the Exodus theme. The teacher should check some resources ahead of time so that the students will be successful in their exploration. Some resources to use are:

    a. The church hymnal—look for hymns or lines of hymns that suggest the Exodus theme.
    b. Books of sermons by Martin Luther King, Jr. and others.
    c. The musical theme from the movie EXODUS.
    d. Stories, poems, movies or novels that have a theme of slavery or lostness followed by struggle for freedom which leads to deliverance and culminates in celebration.
    e. Spirituals, contemporary songs and other music which suggest the Exodus theme.

Students can select one of the resources to search for the theme of Exodus then prepare a way to share the message with the rest of the class. The sharing could be done by:

    a. Involving everyone in singing.
    b. Listening to a recording.
    c. Reading excerpts from poems, sermons or stories.
    d. Illustrating through drawings, slides or a collage the essence of the Exodus theme.

Step Five/Discussion

A discussion could be led by the teacher which might include responses to questions such as:

    a. What are some examples of Exodus experiences that persons have today?
    b. What do you think are some of the essential feelings and emotions of persons who experience Exodus events in their lives?

c. Compare the similarities and differences of the Exodus experiences of the Hebrews with the crucifixion-resurrection experiences of the Christians.

d. Of the passages that you read, which one is most meaningful to you? Why?

e. How would you explain to someone else who has not studied this material the importance of the Exodus experience for the people of God—then and now?

9 *Give Thanks to the Lord*

INTRODUCTION

The activities in this session could be used anytime during the year but they would be especially appropriate for a session near Thanksgiving in November. Depending upon how much time and how many students you have, you may not be able to do all of these activities in one session.

Step One/Setting the Stage

To begin the session we want to focus on some biblical passages that emphasize thankfulness. If Concise Concordances are available for students to use, they could search for passages that reflect something related to each of the following topics:

A. Thankfulness regarding personal experiences. . . . .
B. Thankfulness regarding relationships with God. . . .
C. Thankfulness regarding relationships with others. . . .
D. Thankfulness regarding the world and possessions. . . .

If time is limited or Concordances are not available, the teacher may prepare a list of Psalms for students to look at that would help them to respond to the above four topics.

Psalms 21, 27, 30, 34, 100, 104, 111, 136 and 138

After finding passages related to thankfulness, spend a few minutes comparing notes and discussing one or two questions:

A. What does it mean to be thankful to the persons who wrote these Psalms?
B. Which of the passage means the most to you?

Step Two/The Survival Game

We often take many things for granted. We take so much for granted that we often forget to be thankful. In this game we will focus on the values we attribute to much that we take for granted.

A. Read the introduction together.
B. Remind the persons that they can also take what they are wearing and have in their pockets.
C. The situation is imaginary. The remote place has water, trees, and cultivatable land.
D. Persons rank the 12 items by themselves for themselves.

Be sure to reproduce the following worksheet so that each student will have one.

The Survival Game

The Situation

There is an impending, catastrophic disaster that is expected to occur in the very near future so that life as we know it in the United States may come to an end. You have been chosen to be a part of a select group of persons who are going to travel to a remote place in order to start a new community and continue civilization. The following are some things you would like to take with you. You are not sure you will be able to take everything so, in case you have to leave something behind, you need to rank these things in the order of their importance for you.

Rank the following items from highest to lowest priority, #1 for highest and #12 for lowest.

_____ A variety of seeds for fruits and vegetables.

_____ A collection of books of poems, novels, biographies, and short stories.

_____ Several animals of your choice

_____ A medicine chest with medicines and first aid equipment

_____ Some basic tools like hammers, saws, shovels, hoes, axes, etc.

_____ A sewing machine, sewing materials, and fabrics.

_____ A windmill and electric generator

_____ Some other books like medical encyclopedia, farming and construction manuals, the Bible, and a Dictionary.

_____ A battery operated radio and tape recorder with a collection of 50 selected tape recordings and also some blank tapes.

_____ Several musical instruments and books of music.

_____ A small chest of odds and ends like thread, needles, eating and cooking utensils, candles, rope, etc.

_____ One other item of your choice. What is it? _____

Step Three/Group Interaction

Survival is not just personal survival but group survival. The group (6 to 10 persons) has to decide which items they would take if they were the group selected to survive.

The group can only take *nine* of the twelve items.

After the group(s) have spent 5-10 minutes deciding what to select, interrupt them with an "emergency message" that states they can now take only *seven* items.

Call "time" after about fifteen minutes.

Step Four/Reflection and Discussion

Use questions such as the following to guide a discussion that will help the students to reflect on the experience of the survival game.

1. What assumptions were you making when you made individual choices? When you made group choices? Why?
2. What values are reflected by your top choices?
3. What are some things we take for granted in our everyday lives?
4. What are some things for which you are thankful?
5. How can you express your thankfulness?
6. Read a passage of Scripture—Matthew 6:19-34. What are some connections between that passage of scripture and our playing and discussing the Survival Game?

Step Five/Writing a Prayer

We started the session reading Psalms (many of which were prayers) so now we will close the session by writing some of our own prayers using a form such as the one provided.

A Prayer of Thanksgiving

O God, creator of all the world:

I thank you for. . . .

I pray to you that. . . .

I wish. . . .

There are times when I feel. . . .

---

10 *King David's Important Relationships*

INTRODUCTION

David was one of the most important persons in Old Testament history; perhaps second only to Moses. The biblical material relevant to David is extensive. One must understand something about David in order to make sense of all the references that the New Testament writers made to David when they wrote about the place of Jesus in the history of God's people, Israel. Because there is so much material in the Bible which focuses on David there are several possible ways to approach the study of David:

1. Chronologically, focusing on the sequence of all the important events in his life.
2. Theologically, focusing on his contributions to the religious life and expectations of the people.
3. Militarily, dealing with his work as soldier and king.
4. Biographically, searching for all the personality traits and characteristics that make him the person he was.

We are going to use a fifth approach for our study of David. We are going to focus on some of the important relationships David had during his lifetime. There are other relationships than the ten we are to study, but perhaps these are the most important ones.

Objectives

At the end of the session(s) the students should be able to:
1. Recall five or more significant relationships that David had with others.
2. Describe in some detail one particular relationship that David had with another.

3. Find key passages of scripture which focus on relationships that David had with others.
4. Express in a creative way some of the feelings and values that were present in a relationship that David shared with another party.

Step One/Important Relationships with David

Each student will select one of the following names to be the focus for some research about David. Persons who select the same name can work together or separately, depending on the resources available, the teacher's directions, or their own preference.

1. Jesse
2. Saul
3. Jonathan
4. Goliath
5. Bathsheba
6. Nathan
7. Absalom
8. Solomon
9. God
10. The Philistines

"O my son! My son Absalom!"
(2 Samuel 19.4)

Step Two/Search in Scripture and other Resources

Using Bible Concordances, Dictionaries, Atlases, Encyclopedia, and other resources search for Bible passages and information about the relationship between David and the other party. Read as much in the Bible as there is time available and search in at least two or three of the other resource books.

With younger students with limited time the teacher may want to preselect passages of Scripture related to each of the names.

Step Three/Questions to Guide the Search

As students are searching for relevant Scripture passages and using other resources, they could use the following questions to guide them:

1. What were the circumstances of the coming into relationship between David and the other?
2. What do we learn about David, and about the other party, through the way they related to each other?
3. What are some of the strengths and weaknesses of their relationship?
4. What influence do you think the other party had on David's life and in who he became?

Step Four/Write A Letter

Put yourself in David's place. Write a letter to the other party in the relationship. Express some of your thoughts and feelings about yourself and toward the other. Comment in the letter on your (David's) feelings about one or two of the events that occurred in your life together.

Step Five/Share the Letters

Be sure there is time for persons to share their letters with each other. This is an important step. Before reading the letters, persons should share some of the essential information they discovered related to David and his relationship with the other party.

11 Amos

INTRODUCTION

In this section we are going to present a series of ten activities that could be used to plan a whole unit of three or four sessions on Amos. The same activities could be devised to use in a set of Learning Centers. It is not expected that any teacher or group of students would do all of these activities.

Some or all of these activities related to Amos could be used as models for planning teaching activities to focus on other persons, events, or themes in the Bible.

Activity One/Introduce Amos

By using a set of questions and several helpful resources, students could become acquainted with some of the essential facts related to Amos.

    A. What does the name Amos mean?
    B. Where did Amos live?
    C. What kind of work did Amos do before becoming a prophet?
    D. What is the meaning of the words "prophet" and "prophecy"?
    E. Where did Amos do his prophesying?
    F. What were some of the main points of Amos' message?
    G. How did persons respond to Amos' message?
    H. What were some of the political, social, religious concerns·or actions of the people in Amos' day?

Activity Two/An Outline of the Book of Amos

Skimming the book of Amos, students could search for the missing parts to the following outline of the book of Amos.

Introduction: Amos, chapter 1, verses _____ and _____

First Section: Amos, chapter 1, verse _____ to chapter 2, verse _____

Eight oracles spoken against:

    1. _____   5. _____

    2. _____   6. _____

    3. _____   7. _____

    4. _____   8. _____

Second Section: Amos, chapters 3, 4, 5, and 6

Words of the Lord spoken against. . . .

_____ chap. 3, vs 1

_____ chap. 4, vs 1

_____ chap. 5, vs 1

_____ chap. 6, vs 1

Third Section: Amos 7:1-9:8

    Four visions of Amos

    1. _____   3. _____

    2. _____   4. _____

(Amos 7:10-17, a separate part describing Amos' encounter with the priest _____ .)

The ending: Amos _____:_____-_____

Activity Three/Overview of the Book of Amos

The focus of this overview of Amos will be on the political, social and religious situation and practices in the time of Amos.

A. Divide chapters 2 to 8 among the persons in the group. One or more persons could focus on each chapter.

B. Each person skims a selected chapter searching for verses that give clues to the social, political and religious life of Israel in Amos' day.

C. An example of what we mean is Amos 2:6&7 "They sell the innocent for silver and the poor for a pair of shoes." Look for passages that suggest actions and attitudes of the people of Israel.

D. Share among all the participants to see how much was discovered in the seven chapters.

Activity Four/A Song: Prepare You for the Day

On the album MEET THE PROPHETS by Fr. George Montegue (see Bibliography for availability) there is a song about Amos, "Prepare You for the Day."

A. Listen to the introduction to the recording and to the song.

B. Listen to the song a second time. This time have the words of the song visible so that persons can follow the words as they listen.

C. Skim through the book of Amos searching for passages of Scripture that are the basis for the words of the song.

D. After the song discuss briefly a couple of questions:
1. What are some feelings you have about Amos or about God after listening to this song?
2. If you had a chance for a conversation with the song writer, what are some questions you would like to ask him? Or, what are some comments you would make?

Activity Five/Words of the Lord to Israel

Amos' words, especially in chapters 3 to 6, were words of judgement against the people of Israel. Prophets speak words of judgement today.

A. Read Amos' words of judgement and discuss why you think Amos spoke so boldly to the people.

B. Encourage persons to imagine *themselves* speaking as Amos. Amos was speaking words of the Lord to Israel, but we want to speak words of the Lord to the church.

C. Persons can direct their words to the official board of the local church, to an agency or executive of the denomination, or to an ecumenical body.

D. Take time for each person to identify some actions or attitudes they want to address. Then write, or speak in a tape recorder, a couple of paragraphs that would represent their "words of the Lord" to the church body they chose.

Still you did not come back to me.
(Amos 4.9)

Activity Six/Amos' Understanding of Yahweh

A. Skim through the chapters of Amos searching for examples of statements that represent some of Amos' concepts of and beliefs in Yahweh, his God.

B. Share these findings by completing the sentence, "Amos believed in Yahweh as a God who. . . ."

C. Move from Amos to the present and our own beliefs in God. Each person write down five to eight short sentences that state some of his/her beliefs about God. We are not looking for a "right set" of statements. Whatever a person writes is okay. Each statement starts with, "I believe. ."

D. In pairs, share with each other the five to eight statements.

E. A question to discuss: If we took our beliefs as seriously as Amos took his and applied them to our words and our actions, what would happen?

Activity Seven/Looking for Justice in the Newspaper

One of the key concepts of Amos is the concept of justice. It is necessary to set the stage by reading, interpreting and discussing justice in the book of Amos before discussing justice in our society.

A. Read in Amos and then use some Bible Commentaries to gain some background on the following passages:
   Amos 5:6-15, 5:21-24, and 6:1-12

B. Some questions to discuss:

   1. What do you think Amos means when he speaks of justice and injustice?
   2. What are some other passages in the Bible that focus on justice?
   3. Even though the word justice appears only four times in Amos, in what sense does the theme of justice permeate the whole book?

C. Leader needs to bring several newspapers to class for the participants to use. It is suggested that the Sunday paper may NOT be the best one to bring.

D. Participants each take a section of a newspaper to browse through looking for items that seem to represent something about justice and/or injustice. Items may be found in articles, editorials, letters to the editor, ads, or even the comics. Remind the participants that this *is not* the time to catch up on reading a paper they missed. This *is* time to skim, browse, look quickly for appropriate items that focus on justice or injustice.

E. Cut or tear the items from the paper so that they are visible and can be shared.

F. Gather in groups of three to five persons. Each person select *one* item from the newspaper to be shared with the others. Each one shares an item by responding to the question, "Why did you choose the item you did and in what ways does it relate to the concept of justice?"

Activity Eight/A Filmstrip on Amos

A filmstrip focused on Amos could be used in several different ways: (See Bibliography for availability)

A. Filmstrip could be used early in a unit to present general background on Amos.

B. Filmstrip could be used without the narration to focus a discussion as the teacher raises questions in response to selected frames.

C. Students could use script from the filmstrip as a basis for creating their own write-on or scratch slides.

D. Students could use filmstrip without script as basis for writing their own narration.

Activity Nine/Prosecution and Defense of Amos

A. Consider Amos, the times, his writings, etc.

B. Prepare a list of charges against Amos.

C. Prepare a list of reasons for supporting and affirming Amos.

D. Half of the group prepares an argument for his prosecution, the other half prepares an argument for his defense.

E. Present arguments in a mock trial with teacher or someone else as the judge.

Activity Ten/Responding Personally to Amos

In order for persons to summarize some of their learnings from the book of Amos and to express some of their own feelings and ideas, they could do one of the following writing activities:

A. Write a letter *to* Amos. Assume a contemporary *or* a biblical time-frame. Express to Amos your responses to his book.

B. Write a letter to a friend telling him/her about Amos and his book. Give your friend some reasons why he/she should read the book of Amos.

C. Write out a series of questions you would like to ask Amos if you could interview him. Find someone else who wrote questions and interview each other as you role-play Amos being interviewed.

D. Write a poem that expresses some of the ideas and feelings in the book of Amos.

E. Write a letter as if you were Amos. Write to some designated group to deliver to them a message that represents the "words of the Lord" for that time, place, and situation.

12 *Prayers in the Bible*

INTRODUCTION

Prayer is communion with God. Prayer is the expression of praise, confession, thanksgiving and supplication by persons in the privacy of their own selves or in company with others in corporate worship. There are many examples of prayers in the Bible from books of the Old and New Testaments.

In this section there are suggestions of several ways to approach the study of prayers in the Bible. Depending upon time available and the interests or readiness of the students the teacher will choose one way over another. It is also possible that a unit of several sessions could be developed that would include all of these suggestions.

Approach One/Study the Concept of Prayer and Types of Prayers

A beginning activity could be to focus on the general concept of prayer as presented in various parts of the Bible and in the tradition of Christian worship and meditation.

A. Use Bible dictionary, denominational worship books and other resources to study the meaning and place of prayer in the life of Christians and the Church.

B. Analyse the various types of prayers that are used in the weekly liturgy of the church. Identify the characteristics of prayers of adoration or praise, confession, thanksgiving petition and supplication.

C. Browse through several books of prayers to select a style of praying that is preferable to each person. Each person choose one prayer that represents something of real personal feeling and value. Share that prayer with the whole group.

D. Write brief prayers that represent one or more of each of the five categories:
Praise—recognizing who God is.
Confession—recognizing who I am.
Thanksgiving—expressing appreciation for all that God is and does in spite of my unworthiness.
Petition—identifying needs of others.
Supplication—praying for myself.

Approach Two/Prayers in Psalms

The Book of Psalms includes hymns, creedal statements, litanies, stories, and prayers. There are many types of prayers expressing many different needs and feelings. This book is a rich devotional resource for a person's own prayer life.

A. In the Good News Bible each Psalm is identified by a heading. By quickly skimming over the headings, it is easy to identify the theme and style of each Psalm.

B. Look for Psalms that reflect each of the five categories: Praise, Confession, Thanksgiving, Petition, and Supplication.

C. Search for one or two Psalms that express one's own feelings and needs at the moment.

D. If available, use the Book PSALMS/NOW by Leslie Brandt to read and compare this contemporary transformation of a Psalm with the translation of the Psalm in the Revised Standard Version and/or the Good News Bible.

E. Prepare a brief liturgy that would be composed completely of Psalms. The liturgy could include:
Prayer of Adoration—

Hymn of Praise—(select a Psalm that has been transposed to music)
Prayer of Confession—
Prayer of Thanksgiving—
Proclamation of the Word—
Hymn of Affirmation
Prayer of Petition
Closing Litany.

When you lift your
hands in prayer. . .
(Isaiah 1.15)

Approach Three/Jesus Prays

There are a number of examples in the Gospels where Jesus takes time to pray and speaks about prayer.

A. Locate six to ten passages that show Jesus praying. Students could find their own passages by using a Bible Concordance and Dictionary.

Or, the students could select from the following passages:

1. Luke 3:21, 5:16, 6:12, 9:16, 9:18, 9:28&29, 10:21, 11:1, 22:39ff., 23:34, 23:46, 24:30

2. John, chap. 17

3. Matthew 6:5-15

B. Each student selects one or more of the passages and reads the verses before and after in order to understand the context of the reference to Prayer.

C. During and after reading the passage it is helpful to focus on several questions:
1. What was the occasion of Jesus praying?
2. What does the event of praying or the prayer itself teach us about Jesus?
3. Were there any results from the praying?

D. Students could imagine themselves as one of the disciples alongside Jesus while he is praying. They could write their own prayers in their own words as if they were praying at the same time and place as Jesus.

Additional Suggestions

After doing one of the Approaches, the class might agree on a strategy to incorporate prayer into the life of the students. If we are concerned in Christian education about application of what is "learned" to how we live, then it seems we need to move from learning about prayer to making prayer an important part of our lives. The teacher can begin this process by making prayer a normal and important part of the class session, which provides some opportunities for students to hear the teacher pray and to practice themselves the art of praying.

Some suggestions might be:

1. A box in which students put their "prayer requests". These requests can be for anything and should be signed with their names. Other students who wish to participate may draw a request from the box and take it home with the understanding that they will pray for that person each day of the week.

2. Students might identify persons in the congregation to pray for. A prayer can be offered in class for that person and/or students might commit themselves to praying for that person during the week.

3. Students might identify problems in the church, class, or in town that need to be prayed about. They might write prayers in response to these concerns. If the prayers concern the church or congregation then the prayer might be used in the worship service.

4. Students might develop the use of a "prayer diary" in which students can write their prayers. These may be shared or not, but time would be given each week for students to write at least one prayer.

5. The class might decide to set aside a short period of time at the beginning or end of each class session which would be devoted to prayer. This time might be an opportunity to offer prayers of adoration, or asking God's guidance during the class period, or asking God's care of the members of the class during the week. It may be led by the teacher or the students. Or, this time may be a longer period of time where some specific teaching strategies are used to involve students in one of the above activities.

As in other activities used in the classroom, it is important that students not be "put on the spot" but have the right to "pass". Not all students will feel comfortable praying out loud in front of the class. A class can get bogged down if every member of the class is expected to pray aloud and persons can be discouraged from praying if they feel they have to quickly make up something in order to have something to say when it is their turn. That is not prayer. Since prayer is very personal, the privacy of students needs to be respected.

13 *Themes in the Gospel of Mark*

INTRODUCTION

We could approach the study of the Gospel of Mark in several ways:

    A. Chapter by chapter, verse by verse, to gain as much understanding of Mark's gospel as possible.

    B. Comparing parallel passages with other Gospels to discover the similarities and differences between Mark and the other Gospels.

    C. Critical-historical analysis of the message(s) in Mark, the authorship, dating, audiences, etc.

    D. Themes or key concepts that provide a focus in order to do an overview of the whole gospel.

In this section we are going to outline a process by which a whole class could focus on several themes present in the gospel of Mark.

Step One/Present an Overview of Mark

Before the class begins its exploration on several themes in the gospel of Mark, it would be helpful for the teacher, a guest speaker, or the pastor to make a brief presentation that would introduce some of the general background of Mark. That presentation could include such points as:

    A. Authorship: No internal reference to a particular Mark. Tradition attributes authorship to John Mark—a companion of Peter. Probably written by a gentile Christian. Believed to have been written in Rome.

    B. Style: A message of good news—salvation—a gospel. Written in common, everyday

Greek. Emphasis upon the actions of Jesus rather than on his words and teachings and interpretations of them. Jesus is presented as a man of action and authority.

C. Outline:
    I. Introduction (1:1-13)
    II. Jesus' ministry in Galilee (1:14-9:50)
        A. About the Sea of Galilee
        B. Wider journeys
    III. From Galilee to Jerusalem (10:1-52)
    IV. The last week in Jerusalem (11:1-15:47)
        A. Events and encounters (11:1-12:44)
        B. Apocalyptic discourse (13:1-37)
        C. Passion Narrative (14:1-15:47)
    V. The empty tomb (16:1-8)
    VI. Appearances and ascension (16:9-20)
        (two old endings to the gospel)

Step Two/Select a Theme to Explore

Each person selects one theme to be his/her focus of study. If there are twelve or fewer in the class the teacher may want to limit the themes to two or three instead of using all six. It works best when three or four persons select the same theme. Some possible themes are:

A. Miracles   D. Names and Titles of Jesus
B. The Woman   E. Jesus' Encounters with Authorities
C. The Disciples   F. Responses of the crowds to Jesus.

Took her by the hand, and. . . .
the fever left her.
(Mark 1.31)

Step Three/Work in Small Groups

Small groups are formed by persons who selected the same theme. To do their work quickly, the group could do the following:

A. Divide the sixteen chapters among the persons in the group.
B. Each person skims his/her chapters looking for references to the group's theme.
C. Keep some notes on what is discovered.
D. Share among members of the small group what was found and discuss together some of the insights, questions, or discoveries that arise from the reading and discussing.

Step Four/Interaction of Themes and Groups

Each person joins with two other persons from different small groups exploring other themes. This is a time for sharing some general insights with each other regarding their several themes.

A concluding question to discuss could be: "As you focused on your theme, what did you learn about Jesus?"

14 *Names and Titles of Jesus*

INTRODUCTION

In section 13 we presented a way the whole class could work on several themes to gain an overview of the gospel of Mark as reflected through those themes. In this section we want to zero in on one of the themes, "Names and Titles of Jesus", to show how the whole class could spend their time on one theme. The activities in this section plus some of the suggested spinoffs will require two or three sessions.

The teacher could select one or more gospels to be the focus of study. The choice of which gospel, or how many, would depend upon the number of students in the class. The sequence of activities would be the same no matter how many or which gospel is chosen.

Step One/Assign the Chapters

If there are ten to sixteen younger students, use the gospel of Mark. Divide the chapters among the students so that each will read or skim one or more chapters.

Step Two/Read or Skim the Chapters

Older youth or adult students will be able to skim the chapter quickly. Younger students will have to read the chapters line by line. Skimming is a skill of an older learner. That means that if the class is of older students then more than one chapter could be assigned to each.

The students skim or read looking for only one topic, names *and* titles of Jesus. Each name or title is written down on a piece of note paper.

Step Three/Make Composite List

After students have completed their searching for names and titles then they put all of them together to make a composite list on a chalkboard, newsprint, or overhead transparency. It is essential for this composite list to be visible and available to all the students.

Step Four/Follow-Up Activities

There are several possible follow-up activities. Choose which one(s) to use depending upon time available and abilities of the students.

   A. Organize the names and titles by gospels to see what is unique to each gospel and what they all have in common.

   B. Organize the names and titles into categories and give each category a title and write a summarizing statement for each.

   C. Each student select one name or title to be the focus of his/her further exploration. By using Bible dictionaries, word books, concordances, and commentaries, the students could find answers to questions such as:
      1. What is the meaning or definition of the name or title?

"Praise the LORD!" (Psalm 150)

2. Are there any Old Testament origins to the name or title? What are they?
3. Who called Jesus by that name or title? Why?
4. What do you learn about Jesus when you look at the times, places and persons where he was called by that name or title?

D. Search for teaching pictures or art prints that present Jesus in a visual way that emphasizes the name or title.

E. Create collages or banners with symbols that represent the name or title in a contemporary way. If banners were created it would be very meaningful to plan with the minister to display the banners on a Sunday when the sermon is focused on Jesus. What a sight it would be if the class were to process with the banners as the congregation sings "All Hail the Power of Jesus' Name."

Jesus Christ is the Messiah * 15

INTRODUCTION

In the previous section we have presented a plan whereby students could explore a variety of names and titles of Jesus. This session focuses specifically on one title of Jesus—Messiah. We are going to explore the concept of Messiah in both Old and New Testaments.

Step One/Questions About Messiah

In order to begin the study of Messiah it may be helpful for the students to raise their own questions and spend a little time searching for some answers.

Use the following statement. Be sure the statement is visible in some way so that the students can read it.

After reading the statement, students are to write down one or two questions that come to their minds.

Messiah

The Jewish people were expecting a messiah to
come to save them. The prophets proclaimed the
coming of a Messiah. The prophets had several
images of what their messiah would look like.
Jesus was identified by many persons as the messiah
they were expecting.

Step Two/A Composite List of Questions

After persons have had a chance to write down a question or two, work together to make a

*This activity is also included in PREPARING FOR THE MESSIAH (Abingdon).

composite list of questions on chalkboard, newsprint, or overhead transparency. The list of questions must be visible so that persons can refer to it as they search for answers.

Step Three/Search for Answers

Spend about ten minutes searching for answers to the questions. Each student selects one or more questions to focus on. Use available resources (see Bibliography for suggestions) to find answers. With some of the questions specific answers may not be possible. Those questions that are more open and analytical may be used as part of the discussion by the whole class. The important thing in this step is for each student to work at his/her own pace and deal with only as many questions as he/she is comfortable with.

After a period of searching, the teacher could guide the class in a time of sharing what they found.

Step Four/Messiah in the Old Testament

A. Each person select *one* of the following passages.

Isaiah 52:l3, 53:6   Isaiah 9:2-7
Micah 5:2-4   Isaiah 40:1-11
Malachi 3:1-5   Jeremiah 31:31-34
Amos 9:11-15

B. Answer the following question from the context of the chosen passage: "What kind of messiah do you think the writer was expecting?"

C. Write the answer on a 3x5 card using one or two sentences.

D. Compare answers among persons with different passages.

Step Five/Messiah in the New Testament

A. Each person select *one* of the following passages:

Matthew 3:13-4:11   Mark 8:31-38
Matthew 11:1-19   Mark 11:1-11
Matthew 17:1-13   Luke 4:16-28
Mark 2:1-12   John 10:1-21
                        John 13:1-20

"This is my body."
(Mark 14.22)

B. Answer the following question from the context of the chosen passage: "In what ways do you think the actions and/or teachings of Jesus caused persons to think of him as a messiah?"

C. Write the answer on a 3x5 card.

D. Compare answers among persons with different passages.

Step Six/Compare Old and New Testament Concepts

At a table of six or more persons there should be at least six 3x5 cards with answers for each of the Testaments. Place the cards in two columns down the middle of the table putting all the New Testament cards in one column and the Old Testament cards in a parallel column. Compare the cards to see the differences or similarities between the concept of the Messiah that was to come and the one that did come.

A question to discuss: "What kind of messiah are we looking for?"

Step Seven/Respond Creatively

Each person can use a large sheet of drawing paper. Draw a line down the middle. Use one side for the Old Testament and the other side for the New. Draw a picture, symbol or line drawing to represent an Old Testament image of Messiah and then draw a New Testament image.

If some students do not want to draw, perhaps they could write a poem, or construct symbols from pipe cleaners or thin wire, or create an image on an overhead transparency.

Be sure to allow time for persons to share what they have created.

Portraits of Jesus 16

Objectives

At the end of the session the students should be able to:

1. Compare a variety of artistic expressions of Jesus stating the uniqueness of each.

2. State in a brief verbal presentation why there are such a variety of expressions of what Jesus is like.

3. Express in an art form their own personal "portrait" of Jesus.

Teacher Preparation

Prior to the class session, the teacher needs to secure a wide variety of artistic representations of the physical appearance of Jesus. The following sources should be helpful:

1. Church and community libraries.
2. Church school teaching picture file.
3. Religious art anthologies or prints from art store or museum.
4. Christmas cards.

Students will need other resources and materials for this session including New Testaments, magazines, and creative art materials.

If equipment and resources are available, the teacher should preview the following filmstrips to consider their potential usefulness:

ANOTHER FACE OF JESUS
CHRIST IN THE ART OF JAPAN
CHRIST IN THE ART OF AFRICA

"I saw the Spirit come down like a dove." (John 1.32)

While the students are arriving, there could be available on several tables displays of books and paintings for them to browse with. Also, a filmstrip projector could be set up on a table for students just to look at one or more of the selected filmstrips.

Step One

Give each student a sheet of paper and pencil with the following instructions:

"In three minutes think of as many words as possible which you could use to describe the physical appearance and the personality characteristics of Jesus. Make a list of words or short phrases that tell what Jesus was like based on your impressions and imagination from hearing and reading about him."

After the students have had time to write down as many words as possible, they can exchange papers. Then make a composite list on chalkboard, overhead transparency, or newsprint. Have the students read the words from the lists they made up. By exchanging papers all words will be offered without someone thinking his words are silly or wrong.

Step Two

When the composite list is completed, spend some time arranging the list in a variety of categories. Let students suggest the categories or, if group is large enough, work in small groups, report their categories. Categories should appear that suggest physical features, actions, feelings, and others.

Ask the question: *"What does out list say about Jesus or about our ways of looking at Jesus?"* Students will probably suggest that everybody had different impressions and that Jesus must have been a many faceted person.

Step Three

Give each student a magazine or two (People, Time, Newsweek and other magazines with an abundance of pictures would be preferable).

Suggest that the students look through the magazines to select **one picture** and **one word** that "says" for them something about their impressions of Jesus.

Step Four

After they have selected their words and pictures, have the students keep these in hand as they browse through the display of art paintings, books, Christmas cards, etc. to see if they can find a painting or picture which would be comparable to their previous selection.

This will help them to be analytical of the paintings and pictures. They will discover that the artists had points of view and impressions they were seeking to communicate.

When they have made the selection, they can mount their pictures and words on a poster, bulletin board, box, or other suitable surface. The paintings or pictures could also be mounted. Look analytically at the collection of pictures to see what it says about Jesus.

Step Five

After discussing impressions of Jesus and selecting pictures and words, the students may be ready for one or more of the following activities:

A. To see a filmstrip as suggested above under teacher preparation.

B. To work in a media of paint, clay, or chalk to express some of their feelings and impressions of Jesus.

C. To write a poem about Jesus.

D. To compare key passages in the four Gospels which express some significant characteristics of Jesus that are unique to each Gospel.

E. To do a word study on several key descriptive words about Jesus: Teacher, Christ, King, Lord, Messiah, Son of God; Son of Man, Savior.

Persons Who Met Jesus 17

INTRODUCTION

In this session persons will become intimately involved with a person who met Jesus. In the process of the several steps the participants will move from gaining some *information* about a person to *interpreting* what they discover about the person to *identifying* in a personal way with the person who met Jesus.

The only materials needed are: one blank name tag and one copy of the GOOD NEWS BIBLE or GOOD NEWS FOR MODERN MAN for each person.

Step One/Select a Person

Printed on a chalk board, newsprint, or overhead transparency will be the following six names:

    Nicodemus   Andrew   Mary Magdalene   Zacchaeus   Matthew   Thomas

Each participant selects one name and prints that name on his/her name tage and attaches the name tage to his/her clothing.

Don't worry how many choose which name if you have fifteen or more students. If you have a smaller class then you could use fewer names or prepare name tags ahead of time for the students to select. It works best if at least two students select each name.

Step Two/Search for Information

Use index in GOOD NEWS BIBLE, a Bible Dictionary, Concordance and/or other resources to search for Scripture passages in order to gain some information about the person that was chosen.

As persons read they should seek to answer the following three questions:

    A. Why did the person and Jesus meet?
    B. What happened to the person because of his/her encounter with Jesus?
    C. What feelings do you think the person had toward Jesus?

He was a little man
(Luke 19.3)

Step Three/Compare Notes

Each participant meets with two or three others who chose the same person. In just a few minutes they compare notes regarding what they found and their answers to the three questions. This step is important so that everyone will be prepared for the next step. Keep the groups small. Be sure some time is spent discussing the third question.

Step Four/Sharing Impressions of Jesus

Participants put themselves in the places of the Bible persons they chose. They circulate among the group to find two or three persons who have *different* Bible names. They will spend about five minutes sharing their impressions of Jesus. They talk in the first-person about the influences Jesus had on their lives and their feelings toward Jesus.

Step Five/Wrap Up Discussion

Spend a few minutes discussing the experiences of the session and relating the activities to the everyday experiences of being followers of Jesus.

If no resources are available to guide the search for information about the persons who met Jesus, then a chart with the following passages could be printed.

Biblical passages related to the following persons

ANDREW	Matthew 4:18-20 10:1-15 Mark 14:3ff John 1:35-42, 6:1-15 and 12:20-26
MARY MAGDALENE	Matthew 27:55-61 and 28:1-10 Mark 15:42-47 and 16:1-8 Luke 8:1-3 John 20:1-18
MATTHEW (also called Levi)	Matthew 9:9-13 and 10:1-15 Mark 2:13-17 Luke 5:27-32
NICODEMUS	John 3:1-21, 7:45-52, and 19:38-42
THOMAS	Matthew 10:1-15 John 11:1-16, 14:1-14, and 20:24-29
ZACCHAEUS	Luke 19:1-9

"Look at my hands. . .stop your doubting and believe!" (John 20.27)

Discovering the Twelve 18 Disciples

Objectives

At the end of the session the students should be able to:

1. Identify by name and unique characteristics six of the twelve disciples.
2. Use the footnotes and cross-reference notes in locating parallel passages in the Gospels.
3. Use profitably three of the resource books.

Step One

With students sitting at tables facing the chalkboard or overhead projector, the teacher says: "Let's make a list of the names of the twelve disciples." Usually the students respond with names which are not among the 12 disciples; i.e., Paul, Mark, Luke, Moses, etc. Keep prompting them to mention names without any discussion of whether the name is right or wrong. Often the class will end up with more than 12 names on the board and usually four or five of the disciples names are omitted.

Step Two

Now go back over the names one at a time. Discuss each one to see if the students have a good reason for leaving the name on the board or not. If they decide to remove a few names, erase them. Often there are fewer than 12 names remaining.

Ask the question: "How can we find out the correct names of the 12 disciples and learn something about them?

Step Three

Suggest that the students work for a few minutes to see if they can find the names of the twelve disciples any place in the Bible. Allow them to work for only a few minutes then ask if anyone has found the verses.

Have available a Bible for each person. Also, several copies of YOUNG PEOPLE'S BIBLE DICTIONARY and BIBLE ENCYCLOPEDIA FOR CHILDREN are necessary, and there should be copies of a Concordance.

Note: Complete listings of the twelve disciples are found in the following places: Matthew 10:1-4, Mark 3:13-19, Luke 6:12-16 and Acts 1:13

Step Four

When one person suggests one of the places where the disciples are mentioned, have the whole class turn to that passage.

Then make four columns on the chalk board. Identify the first column with the passage that is being referred to. Have the person read all the names and copy them on the board as he reads.

At once they left their nets.
(Mark 1.18)

Now, have the class look at the cross-reference listings at the bottom of the page. (Be sure to use Bibles that have these cross-reference listings). Explain how the dark numbers refer to the passage on that page and the lighter numbers refer to similar passages in other books. Then look up these references one at a time and list them in the remaining columns parallel to the first listing.

Ask: "What observations would you make now that you see these four lists side by side?"

Allow time for the students to think, reflect, and express their ideas and observations.

Be sure they notice the following points:

    A. Peter is listed first . . . . the most prominent of all the 12.
    B. Judas is listed last. . . he is regarded as least of the 12 (Remember: these lists were written long after the events that are reported.)
    C. Different names in a couple of places. .due to variety of sources who did not necessarily check with each other.
    D. Only eleven names in the Acts passage. . .after Judas committed suicide and before Mattias was elected (Acts 1:26)

Step Five

Have each student choose the name of one disciple in order to do some research. Try to have all disciples worked on. If there are more than twelve students have a couple of persons do each of the more prominent of the disciples.

Use Bible Dictionaries, Encyclopedia, or a book PEOPLE OF THE BIBLE or other resources that might have information about the disciples. A Concordance or the Index in the GOOD NEWS BIBLE will give specific verse or page references for each of the disciples.

Look up several verses to find information on each of the disciples.

Step Six

Plan for each student to report to the class sharing his/her research so that all of the students will gain some understanding and appreciation for all twelve of the disciples.

Step Seven

As a few summarizing questions:

    A. What do you think of these disciples as a group?
    B. What made them so special?
    C. If you were going to start a movement like Jesus did, what kind of persons would you pick to be your disciples?
    D. Who are some of Jesus' disciples today?
    E. In what ways are you a disciple?

Some Other Activities

If you have time in the session or plan to extend the focus on the disciples to include another session or two, there are some other activities that could be planned.

    A. Use a cassette tape from the FAITH ALIVE series by Thesis Tapes (Call of the Disciples). This particular tape focuses specially on the 12 disciples and their relationships with Jesus and each other. (See Bibliography for source)

    B. Present the filmstrip "JESUS AND THE TWELVE DISCIPLES" by Annie Vallatton (Illustrator for the GOOD NEWS BIBLE). The Leader's Guide with the filmstrip will suggest some ways to use it with the class. (See Bibliography for the source).

    C. Create some games or other activities that help to reinforce the names and other characteristics of the twelve disciples.

Peter: Fisherman and 19 Apostle

INTRODUCTION

When the listings of the twelve apostles are compared side by side, we notice in each one that Peter's name appears first. In the traditions surrounding the Apostles, Peter is always identified as the most prominent of the Apostles. There is more information about Peter in the four gospels and the book of Acts than any person other than Jesus.

The outline of this section suggests two ways to approach the study of Peter. Either of the two ways will probably take more than one session of an hour. It would be possible to plan a unit of three or four sessions using all of the suggested activities.

Step One/Characteristics of Persons Like Peter

To arouse some interest in Peter, the teacher could ask the students to think of persons who represent some specific personality traits or characteristics. It is not important to name names but rather to talk about persons in general who have these characteristics.

How many of you know persons who. . . .

    a. Are always the first ones to speak up when the group is asked a question?

    b. Enthusiastic and eager to follow someone who has new ideas or promises exciting adventure?

    c. Sometimes do not stand up for and defend their closest friends because they are fearful?

    d. Make mistakes but somehow are forgiven and recover in order to accomplish great achievements?

    e. Start out as lowly, humble persons but become famous, influential leaders?

After responses to each of the above inquiries, the teacher could ask, "What feelings do you have toward such persons?"

We are going to study about a person who represented all of these characteristics—the Apostle Peter.

Step Two/Questions About Peter

Print the following statement on a poster or sheet of newsprint.

> Peter was a disciple of Jesus Christ.
> His name was not always Peter and he was not
> always a disciple. Jesus gave him the name
> Peter. Peter was a leader and spokesman
> for the disciples. Peter did many important
> things to help establish the early church.

    a. Students read the statement and write down a question or two that could be used to guide further exploration about Peter.

    b. Make a composite list of questions on chalkboard, newsprint, or transparency.

    c. Look at questions to determine which ones would have clear answers as compared to the ones that are more open ended and require interpretation.

Step Three/Explore the Resources

A variety of resources need to be available for students to use. The Index in the GOOD

NEWS BIBLE is a good place to start. Bible Dictionary, Concordance, People of the Bible and other resource books would be very helpful.

    a. Select one question of the list to start with.
    b. Use whatever resources one chooses.
    c. Search for answers to one or more questions.
    d. Write down some notes to be able to share information with others in the class.

Step Four/Brief Discussion

Some questions to ask the whole class to summarize their study of Peter:

    a. How do you feel about Peter?
    b. Why do you think Jesus chose Peter to be a disciple?
    c. What are some feelings the other disciples might have had toward Peter?
    d. What are some questions you would like to ask Peter if you had the opportunity?
    e. In what ways are we like Peter?

"Woman, I don't even know him!"
(Luke 22.56)

Step Five/Some Creative Responses

After the study and discussion about Peter, the students should be ready to express themselves in one of the creative ways suggested below.

    a. Create a series of Write-On Slides to present some important aspects of Peter's life.
    b. Make up a crossword puzzle with diagram and cues all focused on Peter.
    c. Select some pictures from magazines or photo slides to illustrate some of the important events in Peter's life.
    d. Write a letter to Peter asking him some questions and telling him what you think of him.
    e. Work with another student to produce an interview of Peter by a newspaper or radio reporter. The interview could be recorded and shared with the whole class.

Time should be provided for students to share with each other what they have created.

Another Sequence of Activities

Step One/as above

Step Two/Peter's Life in Outline

Slips of paper could be prepared with the following passages of Scripture, or the passages could be listed on a chalkboard. Each student will select one of the passages to work on. If more than one student selects the same passage that is okay as long as all the passages are selected.

    a. Luke 5:1-11. . . .Jesus calls Peter to be a disciple
    b. Matthew 14:22-33. . .Peter tries to walk on water.
    c. Matthew 16:13-20. . .Peter declares Jesus to be the messiah

e. Luke 24:1-12. . .Peter's response to the empty tomb
f. John 21:15-19. . .Jesus and Peter
g. Acts 2:1-16, 32-42. . .Peter at Pentecost
h. Acts 4:1-22. . .Peter and John before the Council
i. Acts 11:1-18. . .Peter's report to the church in Jerusalem

The above nine passages represent important events in Peter's life. Each student focuses on one passage. During and after reading the passage, think about answers to the following questions:

a. What do you learn about Peter's personality and personal characteristics through this passage?
b. What do you think motivates Peter to do what he does or say what he says?

Step Three/Introducing Peter

Each student writes three or four sentences that summarize something about Peter in that episode in his life. The students write in the first-person. In chronological order the students introduce themselves (in the role of Peter) to each other.

After step three you could pick up with step five in the previous strategy presented at the beginning of this section.

Matthew: Tax Collector 20 *and Apostle*

INTRODUCTION

Except for the inclusion of his name in the four listings of the twelve apostles, there is only one other account that gives any background information about Matthew. There are five verses in each of the synoptic gospels that describe Jesus' call of Matthew (called Levi in Mark and Luke) followed by Jesus' encounter with the Pharisees after having a meal in Matthew's house. When we read those five verses it seems almost automatic that Matthew left his tax office to follow Jesus. It seems to me that there is much that is left out of those few verses. Assuming Matthew was as human as we are, there must have been a struggle in his soul to decide whether or not to follow Jesus. The activities in this session attempt to help the students identify with that struggle and to think about the struggles in their own lives when they are deciding whether, and to what extent, to follow Jesus themselves.

This session could follow naturally after either of two other sessions already outlined in this book: "Discovering the Twelve Apostles" and "Persons Who Met Jesus". Also the model of approach that this session represents could be adapted and applied to other persons in the New and Old Testaments.

The success of this session depends upon the availability of a cassette tape from Thesis Tapes (P.O. Box 11724, Pittsburgh, PA 15228). The tape is in the Faith Alive series and is identified by the title "Unit III, 2. Life and Teachings of Jesus: Call of Disciples". One of the episodes on the tape is a dramatic presentation of Jesus' call of Matthew.

Step One/Organize the Group

Before listening to the cassette tape on Matthew, it is necessary to organize the group.

A. Divide the class into smaller groups of four to six persons.

B. In each small group instruct two or three persons to choose to identify with Matthew. The other two or three persons would choose to identify with a reporter. Imagine a reporter from the "Jerusalem Journal" who is an observer of this event of Jesus inviting Matthew to join him in his ministry.

Step Two/Prepare to Listen to the Tape

One more thing needs to be accomplished before listening to the tape. As the "Matthews" and "Reporters" listen to the tape each one needs to have in mind a question to think about as he/she listens.

Question for MATTHEW: What are some good reasons for following and for not following Jesus?

Question for REPORTER: What are some questions you would like to ask Matthew?

Teacher should be sure tape is set at the beginning of the episode. And, the tape should be previewed so that it is clear where to stop the tape.

Step Three/Listening to the Tape

A. Persons listen with their specific questions in mind.

B. The whole episode is about 15 minutes long. However, the tape will be stopped after about three minutes.

C. Stop the tape at the point where Jesus and Matthew have interacted after Jesus' call. At this point in the episode it is not clear whether Matthew will follow or not.

Step Four/Small Group Consultations

For about five minutes two or three Matthews should consult with each other to answer the question: "What are some good reasons for following or not following Jesus?" At the same time two or three Reporters consult with each other to devise some good questions to ask Matthew in an interview.

Step Five/Interviews

After the period of consultation the Reporters should be ready to interview the Matthews. Each reporter will interview a Matthew so that there will be as many interviews happening as there are pairs of students in the class. The interview should not be more than three or four minutes. Reporters should be reminded that this is an interview, not an interrogation.

Step Six/Discussion

Some possible questions for discussion include:

A. How do you feel about Matthew?

B. Was it hard for Matthew to decide to follow Jesus? Why or why not?

C. Why do you think Jesus wanted a person like Matthew to be one of his disciples?

D. What are some examples of struggles in your own life like Matthew's struggle?

Writing a Gospel 21

INTRODUCTION

There are four Gospels in the New Testament. Each Gospel was written by a different person (or persons) at a different time and place for a different audience. The writing of a Gospel was the result of what persons *remembered* and *believed* about Jesus, what they *received* orally or in written form from others and what they *intended* for the persons to whom they were writing. Influencing all of what was written was the work of God's Holy Spirit in the hearts and minds of persons.

Objectives

At the end of this session persons should be able to:

1. Identify three important contributions to the formation of a Gospel.
2. Compare the four gospels in the New Testament and recognize some of their unique differences and their similarities.
3. Express in written form their own beliefs about Jesus.

Step One/Setting the Stage

Before the students begin the process of identifying with the writing of the gospels, it will be important to set the stage with information such as the following.

The word "gospel" means literally "good news". We can refer to the "gospel of Jesus Christ" and mean generally the good news of Jesus' life, death and resurrection and what it means then and today. We can also refer to the four gospels and have in mind the first four books of the New Testament. Each of the four gospels is unique. Each was written by a different author, written for different groups of persons and written to express different interpretations of Jesus.

The Gospels do not include everything that happened. Perhaps even some important things are missing. The Gospels are not just biographies; they are statements of what persons remembered and believed about Jesus. The Gospels were written many years after the events of Jesus' death and resurrection. The first reports and stories about Jesus were transmitted orally. Eventually they were written down and were first referred to as "the memoirs of the apostles."

Finally, in 325 AD, at the Council of Nicea, the Gospels and other books of the New Testament were determined to be the Canon and thus to this day are accepted as Holy Scripture by all Christian churches.

Several factors influenced in a significant way the final writings contained in the Gospels.

1. What the writers themselves remembered and believed about Jesus was of primary importance.

2. What the writers heard from others who were close to Jesus or what they received in written form influenced the shape of their Gospels.

3. Each author was directing his writings to a specific group or groups of persons and what he intended for these persons influenced some of what he wrote.

Today we are going to write a gospel—not as long as the Gospels in the New Testament, but following some of the same steps that their authors took.

Step Two/What is Remembered and Believed

Each person will work at his/her own writing to express what he/she remembers and believes about Jesus.

A. Write down, in ten minutes, as many brief statements as possible that express important memories or beliefs about Jesus. There is no preferred list. Each person just writes from his/her own perspective.

B. Call "time" in ten minutes.

C. Look at all the statements. Select *half* of the number that were written to become part of the Gospel. (Not everything that was remembered and believed was included in the final form of the original gospels.)

Step Three/Receive Statements from Others

A. Two or three persons share their selected statements with each other.

B. Each person selects from the other person(s) one or two statements to add to his/her own list.

Step Four/Consider the Writings of Others

Another resource to use to represent the written memories and beliefs of others is the New Testament Gospel writings themselves. There should be about twelve to fifteen passages of Scripture available. It would be helpful if these passages could be printed on separate sheets of paper so that persons can sort through them and select the ones they want. If you have packs of Scripture Cards* available they would be an excellent resource to use in this activity.

A. Read the twelve to fifteen passages of scripture.

B. Choose five or six to add to the statements already selected. Each person should end up with about fifteen to twenty statements.

C. The passages selected could be similar to or different than the original written statements.

D. Possible Passages Include:

1. Luke 2:8-14
2. Mark 1:14-20
3. Mark 14:22-26
4. Mark 4:30-34
5. Matthew 18:10-14
6. Luke 2:15-20
7. Mark 4:35-41
8. Luke 19:1-10
9. Luke 5:17-26
10. Matthew 6:5-15

11. Mark 8:34-38
12. Matthew 19:13-15
13. Acts 1:6-11
14. Luke 12:22-31
15. Luke 19:28-38
16. Mark 8:1-10
17. Mark 4:1-9
18. Matthew 28:1-10
19. Luke 10:25-37
20. Luke 15:11-24

"Unless you change and become like children. . ." (Matthew 18.3)

Step Five/Identifying Persons to Whom to Write a Gospel

A third factor that influenced the writing of a gospel is the group, or audience, to whom the gospel is addressed. Depending upon the persons to whom we write the gospel may take one form or emphasize some themes over others.

A. As a class, brainstorm six or more possible groups to whom they could write their gospels.

B. The groups should be contemporary and recognizable by particular characteristics so that the students will not have difficulty composing their gospels.

---

*Cards with Line Drawings on one side and Scripture text on the other. Published by the American Bible Society.

Step Six/Writing the Gospels

A. Take about 10-15 minutes to write chapter 1, verses 1-10 of a special, personal gospel.

B. This is just the beginning of a gospel, not the complete gospel.

C. Include as many statements as are desired from the original set, from the other persons, and from the Scriptures.

D. Write in a narrative form.

Step Seven/Sharing and Reflection

A. If the class is small each student could read his/her gospel for the whole class.

B. If the class is large, students could read their gospels to four or five other persons.

C. It is important for students to have an opportunity to reflect on their experiences of writing gospels and to discuss the learnings derived from the activity.

Some questions to consider using:

1. Was it easy or hard to write a gospel? Why?
2. What was the easiest part?
3. What was the hardest part?
4. How do you feel about what you wrote and created?
5. What message would others get about Jesus from reading, hearing, or seeing your gospel?
6. Which was the stronger influence on what you wrote: what you believed or the kinds of persons to whom you were writing?

The Church in Acts and the Epistles 22

INTRODUCTION

Throughout the Book of Acts and the Letters of Paul and others there are many references to the activities of the church in their worship, study and service. In this session we want to identify some of those passages which show the early church in action. Then we want to follow-up with some small group activities that would involve the students in planning a worship service and doing some simple acts of ministry.

Step One/The Work of Our Church

The teacher needs to gather ahead of time samples of the church bulletin, newsletter, annual reports, membership directory, and any other brochures that may be available.

On four sections of a tack board or four large poster boards print a sign for each:

| THE CHURCH WORSHIPS | THE CHURCH SERVES OTHERS |
| THE CHURCH LEARNS | THE CHURCH ORGANIZES |

The students sort through the materials describing the work, programs and services of their church to find examples of articles, announcements or other information that can be classified under one of the above four categories. The items are torn or cut out and mounted under the appropriate signs.

The students could print on cards the names of persons in the church who are related to one or more of the categories and mount those name cards under the appropriate signs.

Step Two/The Work of the Early Church

The following passages of Scripture can also be connected with one or more of the same four categories: 1) The Church Worships, 2) The Church Serves Others, 3) The Church Learns and 4) The Church Organizes.

A. Each passage could be noted on a different 3x5 card.
B. Students select one card at a time.
C. then read the passage in the Bible, and
D. write a one sentence summary of the action described and
E. place the card on the appropriate bulletin board or poster.

Some possible passages include:

1. Matthew 18:21-35   "parable of the Unforgiving Servant"
2. Matthew 22:34-40   "the Great Commandment"
3. Matthew 25:31-46   "the parable of the Final Judgement"
4. Matthew 28:16-20   "the Great Commission"
5. Luke 10:25-37   "the parable of the Good Samaritan"
6. Acts 1:12-14   "They gathered frequently to pray"
7. Acts 1:15-26   "a successor of Judas was chosen"
8. Acts 2:43-47   "believers continued in close fellowship"
9. Acts 4:23-31   "they joined together in prayer"
10. Acts 4:32-37   "no one in the group was in need"
11. Acts 6:1-7   "the appointment of seven helpers"
12. Acts 11:19-30   "the church at Antioch"
13. Acts 18:1-35   "a meeting at Jerusalem"
14. Acts 16:11-15   "worship in Philippi"
15. Acts 17:1-9   "the church in Thessalonica"
16. I Corinthians 11:17-34 "the Lord's Supper"
17. I Corinthians 12:27-31 "the parts of Christ's body"
18. I Corinthians 14:26-40 "order in the church"
19. I Corinthians 16:1-4   "an offering for others"
20. Ephesians 4:1-16   "the work of the church"
21. Colossians 4:2-6   "instructions"
22. I Timothy 2:1-15   "regarding worship"
23. I Timothy 3:1-7   "regarding church leaders"
24. I Timothy 3:8-13   "regarding church helpers"
25. I Titus 2:1-15   "regarding church teaching"

The teacher could select other passages in addition to or instead of these that are listed above. The choice of passages depends upon the number of students, the time available and the objectives of the teacher.

Step Three/A Brief Discussion

With the local church items and Scripture passages categorized, the students will have gained enough information to respond to questions such as:

A. What are some similarities and differences between persons in the church and actions of the church in the first century compared to our church today?

B. If you were to rank the four categories in order of importance, how would you rank them? Why?

C. What are some important actions we can do to fulfill Jesus' expectations of us as his disciples?

D. What are some changes you would recommend in the way the church does its ministry?

"Fellow Jews. . .listen to me!"
(Acts 2.14)

Step Four/Actions of the Church in Small Groups

Students can select one of the four groups to work with in order to accomplish the tasks outlined below.

GROUP A—THE CHURCH WORSHIPS

1. Plan for a 10 minute worship service.
2. Select a Psalm to read as an opening prayer
3. Choose a hymn from the hymn book and sing one or two verses.
4. Read some of the speeches of Peter or Paul in the Book of Acts and select part or all of one speech (or sermon) to read to the class.
5. Write a prayer to close the worship.

GROUP B—THE CHURCH SERVES OTHERS

1. Talk with minister or other church leader to learn about some actions of the church that serve other persons.
2. Ask about some actions that need to be done and are not.
3. Make a list of several possible actions for others that persons in the class could do and select one or two to do.
4. Plan ways to interest others in doing the service to others and ways to accomplish the work.
5. Evaluate what was accomplished. Reflect on the experience by sharing feelings, learnings, disappointments and hopes.

GROUP C—THE CHURCH LEARNS

1. Arrange with a teacher of a class of younger learners to volunteer to help teach that class for one or more Sundays.
2. Meet with the teachers to discuss the possible lesson plans.
3. Decide who is going to do what. Work together in preparing for the teaching.
4. Spend one or more Sundays as helpers to teachers in a church school class.
5. Evaluate the experience by sharing joys and disappointments, learnings and accomplishments, feelings and ideas.

GROUP D—THE CHURCH ORGANIZES

1. Meet with the minister or other church leaders to learn about how the local church is organized, how the denomination is organized and/or how some other churches are organized.
2. Discuss together and with the minister ways the class is related to the organization of the church.
3. Decide on some ways that members of the class can be related to or involved in some of the church organization as an observer or a participant.
4. Spend some time becoming more familiar with and involved in some part of the church's organization.

Step Five/Share Experiences and Learnings

Some means need to be provided by which the participants in each of the above groups and activities can share with each other their experiences and learnings. It may even be possible to involve parents and/or others in such a time of sharing.

23 Paul Speaks to the Crowd

INTRODUCTION

There are many examples in the Book of Acts where Paul speaks out boldly to the people who are present. Some of those occasions are:

A. Paul and Barnabas in Antioch ...... Acts 13:13 to 52
B. Paul in Prison in Philippi .... Acts 16:16 to 40
C. Paul in Athens .... Acts 17:16 to 34
D. Paul at the Temple in Jerusalem .... Acts 21:27 to 22:29

Each of the above examples and many others could be used in the same way as suggested below with one specific event. Before focusing on any one of these events it would be important to have gained some background information about Paul and the setting in which the event occurs.

Step One/Set the Stage

It is important to set the stage by presenting in as dramatic a format as possible the appropriate passage of Scripture. The least effective would be for the students to read the passage for themselves. An effective way would be for someone with dramatic reading ability to record the passage ahead of time then present it in recorded form to the class. Another way would be for the teacher to read the passage with as much dramatic emphasis as possible.

The event we want to focus on is in Acts 21:27-40

"Some Jews from the province of Asia saw Paul in the temple. They stirred up the whole crowd and grabbed Paul. 'Men of Israel!' they shouted. 'Help! This is the man who goes everywhere teaching everyone against the people of Israel, the Law of Moses, and this temple. And now he has even brought some Gentiles into the temple and defiled this holy place!'

"Confusion spread through the whole city, and the people all ran together, grabbed Paul, and dragged him out of the temple. At once the temple doors were closed. The mob was trying to kill Paul when a report was sent up to the commander of the Roman troops that all of Jerusalem was rioting. At once the commander took some officers and soldiers and rushed down to the crowd. When the people saw him with the soldiers, they stopped beating Paul. The commander went over to Paul, arrested him, and ordered him to be tied up with two chains. Then he asked, 'Who is this man, and what has he done?' Some in the crowd shouted one thing, others something else. There was such confusion that the commander could not find out exactly what had happened; so he ordered his men to take Paul up into the fort. They got with him to the steps, and then the soldiers had to carry him because the mob was so wild. They were all coming after him and screaming, 'Kill him!'

"As they were about to take Paul into the fort, he spoke to the commander, 'May I say something to you?'

"I am a Jew, born in Tarsus or Cilicia, a citizen of an important city. Please, let me speak to the people."

"The commander gave him permission, so Paul stood on the steps and motioned with his hand to the people. When they were quiet, Paul spoke to them."

Step Two/Paul's Words to the Crowd

The stage is set. Now is the time for the students to imagine themselves in Paul's place responding to the crowd. Provide enough time for the students to write, or perhaps record, their own words. These statements need not be long and complete. It is mostly important for the students just to think, feel, and respond as they identify with Paul. Even a sentence or two or three would be enough.

Step Three

Provide time for the students to share their statements with each other. Students will be more willing to share their statements if they realize that the teacher will be accepting of whatever they share. We are not looking for outstanding statements. We are looking for students to express whatever they think or feel.

Step Four/Reading from Acts

Read what Paul actually did say to the crowd in Acts 22:1 to 29.

Step Five/Discussion

Some time should be spent discussing the situation of Paul's confrontation with the crowd and the authorities. Some possible questions are:

A. What are some reasons why the people were so upset? How about the soldiers?

B. What do you think were the main points of Paul's statements to the crowd?

C. What are some similarities and differences between the student's statements and Paul's statements?

D. How do you personally respond to what Paul said to the crowd? If you had been there how would you have felt?

24 *Bible Study for Adults in Transition*

INTRODUCTION

The Bible is the sourcebook of **The Story** of our people. In the Bible we find a rich heritage of biographical resources that present persons with the struggles, joys and dreams of their faith and life. There are many ways to study the Bible using the tools of historical, literary and tradition criticism. There is another way to study the Bible which focuses primarily on the personal, relational, life-situational aspects of the biblical material. This approach is not instead of the more technical studies. This approach attempts to enable the Bible to become the living Word of God within the context of persons' own life experiences. To approach the Bible this way is to help adults see the relevance of persons, events, and expressions of feelings in the Bible to their own values, sorrows, joys, fears, and hopes that are present in their transitional experiences. Transition, or passage, through one stage of development to another is an aspect of life for all growing persons, including so-called mature adults.

Karl Olson in his book FIND YOURSELF IN THE BIBLE speaks of this type of Bible study as "Relational Bible Study". For lack of a better title, I too would use that as an appropriate title. By relational Bible study I would mean:

1. The Bible is in one sense a "journal" of the experiences of my people.
2. The people of God known through the patriarchs, prophets, apostles, and especially Jesus Christ are in one sense my relations; they are my ancestors in the faith.
3. In order for the Bible to come alive and speak in this day it must relate to the needs, struggles, and hopes of persons in the present.
4. Since the days when the Bible was written everything has changed except for the basic, human, personal feelings and emotions that people experience in their lives. The Bible very surely relates to the feelings and emotions of people today.
5. We can look to the Bible for many examples of persons in transition. As we identify with these persons perhaps we can relate what happened to them to what is happening to us.

What follows is a series of three approaches for adult Bible study that focus on biblical subjects that speak to adults in transition. In order to conserve space each study is presented in outline form.

Approach One/The Exodus Experience

Introduction: By definition exodus is a process of transition. Led by Moses from Egypt through the wilderness to the promised land, the people experienced all the traumas of transition.

Step 1—Look at the tradition of the Exodus in capsule form
    (I Samuel 12:8, Deuteronomy 26:5-9, and Joshua 24:2-13)
    —Compare these three short versions of the tradition in order to summarize the relationship between Yahweh and the people.
    —Read Psalm 78 for another expression of the tradition.

Step 2—Identify with Moses' at the time of his call.
    —Moses represents a variety of roles, some of which would influence him to stay in Midian (sheepherder, husband, fugitive, reluctant servant, etc.) and others that would influence him to return to Egypt (Israelite, called by God, defender of his people, etc.).
    —After identifying the two categories of roles, persons can work in small groups where some identify with Moses' reluctance to return and others with Moses' strong

committment to Yahweh and his people. After reading the account of Moses' call in Exodus 3, the leader stops with the words "and Moses said to God. . ." The people continue the passage in the form of role play as they respond to God from the perspective of their roles of Moses.

—Reflect on experiences in our lives where we are torn between responding to difficult tasks or playing it safe.

Step 3—Reasons to stay in Egypt vs. going with Moses.
—Consider the situation of the Israelities in Egypt.
—Make a list of good reasons to stay in Egypt.
—Make another list of good reasons to go with Moses.
—Divide into groups of four where two argue to "stay" and two argue to "go".
—Reflect on the experience. Relate to personal experiences that are similar.

Step 4—Trials and Tribulations in the Wilderness.
—Find in the Book of Exodus narrative examples of trials and tribulations in the wilderness journey.
—List each example and answer three questions related to each:
  a. What was the cause of the difficulty?
  b. How did the people respond? Why?
  c. What was God's action on their behalf?
—Persons can work individually to identify recent times in their lives that were like a wilderness experience. Using notebooks, persons can write to describe their wilderness experiences and to respond by answering the same three questions as above.

Step 5—Time for prayer focusing on the experiences of the wilderness journey and God's power to lead persons through stressful times.
—Conclude with Psalm 71 from PSALMS/NOW.

"I am who I am. . .
This is my name forever."
(Exodus 3:14-15)

Approach Two/Abraham's Tent and Solomon's Temple

This Bible study would start by exploring some of the biblical material related to Abraham and Solomon.

It seems to me that Abraham and Solomon symbolize two different approaches to life and to faith. When we compare the characteristics of each we can learn from them and apply their experiences to our own lives.

Abraham embarks on a pilgrimage to a new land.
    Solomon establishes himself in a palace.
Abraham launches out into unknown territory.
    Solomon fortifies a mighty kingdom.
Abraham gathers a few rocks into a pile to build an altar to commemorate his encounter with God.
    Solomon gathers the rarest of woods and stone and the most precious metals to erect a grand and glorious Temple for God's residence.

Abraham walks with God day by day.

Solomon does his duty to God and then forgets his promises.

Abraham searches for God in every tomorrow.

Solomon seeks to memorialize God's actions of yesterday.

Most of us can identify times when our lives are more like the tent and pilgrimage of Abraham and other times when they are more like the palace and temple of Solomon. Using the descriptions of Abraham and Solomon as models for responding to issues of faith and life, persons would be guided to:

1. Recall events in their lives that are like what Progoff calls "Stepping Stones". Stepping stones are those events, experiences, times when a person consolidates his/her place in life and becomes ready for the next move, step, or transition. These events can be listed by the persons for their own personal use.

2. Look at the "stepping stones" to see which ones represent more of an "Abraham style" or more of a "Solomon style".

3. Select a recent or present significant event to focus on to respond to questions such as:
    a. In what sense is this event a transitional experience?
    b. What is being left behind; what is being anticipated?
    c. What are the values of the past that are being continued into the present and future?
    d. What are some ways that the new is very new and different than the past?
    e. What are some ways one can be helped to make the transition more smoothly or more purposefully?

"Choose life."
(Deuteronomy 30.19)

Approach Three/Psalms As A Resource for Persons in Transition

It is possible to spend several weeks or more in a study of Psalms which deals especially with persons in transition. Some possible activities may include:

1. Introduce concepts of tradition, transition, and transformation.
2. Introduce the Book of Psalms.
3. Persons are asked to recall times in their lives when Psalms were meaningfully used. Share the times, share the Psalms.
4. Persons are asked to focus on a favorite Psalm. Share why it is a favorite. Study that favorite Psalm with other translations, a commentary, and other resources to seek to discover new meanings in a familiar Psalm.
5. Persons could be guided to make a list of some of the major, "hinge points" in their lives; times when they were at an intersection and said "yes" to one direction and "no" to another.
6. After listing the "hinge points", persons could select one or more to be their focus and then search through Psalms to find one that speaks to them for that time in their lives.
7. Persons identify some major or minor transitions for which they are presently spending energy thinking, worrying or planning. Search Psalms for one that speaks to the present.
8. Psalms are songs, prayers, statements that express personal feelings. Persons could write their own psalms to reflect their present needs and concerns. These personal psalms could be shared with each other if persons desire to do that.

Using American Bible 25
Society Resources

INTRODUCTION

We started the first of the 20 WAYS of this book by calling attention to the value of the GOOD NEWS BIBLE, a publication of the American Bible Society. In this section we want to conclude the book by recommending some other resources of the American Bible Society and ways to use some of them for teaching the Bible. American Bible Society resources are available from P.O. Box 5656, Grand Central Station, New York, NY 10017.

Individual Gospel, Acts and Psalms Portions

The American Bible Society has prepared in several formats (and prices—from .15 to .65 cents each) small and larger print editions of individual books of the Bible. The books available are: Exodus, Ruth, Job, Jonah, Hosea, Amos, Micah, Proverbs, Ecclesiastes, Psalms, Matthew, Mark, Luke, John, Acts, Galatians, Colossians, Ephesians, and Letters of John. All these books are available in the GOOD NEWS translation.

When a class is studying one book of the Bible, these individual portions can be provided for each member of the class at very little cost. By having inexpensive, individual portions it is possible to do several things with them.

1. Cut them up to make charts, collages, excerpts, and combine them with other printed or visual resources.

2. Mark them up with underline, margin notes, or pencil illustrations to make the study more memorable.

3. Carry them in pockets or notebooks to have readily available for reading and study.

4. Use them alongside one or more other translations of the same book.

"My saving power will rise on you like the sun." (Malachi 4.2)

Good News for New Readers

More than forty little pamphlets, each representing a different story about or by Jesus, are available in five series known as *Good News for New Readers.* They represent an effort by the American Bible Society to provide resources for newly literate adults (also children and youth) to become truly literate regarding the Word of God in the Gospels. Each of the five series is carefully planned to include progressively more advanced material so that persons are able to grow in their reading skills and comprehension. Send for a catalog of the complete listing of the pamphlets which cost less than ten cents each. Each of the pamphlets is illustrated in color with drawings on every page.

These pamphlets can be used in church education in a variety of ways:

1. Give to students to take home as a reminder of their study of the story in church school.

2. Keep a complete set in a box on a shelf in a reading center for students to have available as preclass activity or when they are looking for something else to do.

3. Build learning centers around one or more of the pamphlets.

4. Use for summer Bible study packets prepared for families traveling on vacation.

Cassette Recordings

The complete New Testament and Psalms are available on cassette tape in the GOOD NEWS BIBLE translation. These recordings are of excellent quality, narrated with clarity and feeling. The whole set of sixteen tapes is available for less than $40.00 and would make a significant contribution to the library or resource center of every church.

In addition to making the tapes with a player available to visually handicapped and shut-in persons, they could be used in church education in many ways:

1. Students who cannot read so well can listen to the portion of Scripture that others are reading.

2. Some filmstrips can be accompanied by the narration of Scripture on the tape.

3. Learning Centers could use the tapes for input of biblical content.

4. Taped narration of Scripture could be used in a worship setting.

5. Students could prepare a multi-media presentation with slides, film and/or overhead transparencies using the Scripture on tape as a sound background.

Because the sheep had no shepherd (Ezekiel 34.5)
I myself will be the shepherd of my sheep. (Ezekiel

A Festival of the Bible

A chart and booklet are available that summarizes the development of the English Bible from the original texts to the present. These resources would make an excellent contribution to a youth or adult class' study of the history of the Bible. It would be possible to combine the study with planning a program or project that involves a larger segment of the church membership. Bible Sunday or any Sunday of the year could be designated as a time for a Festival of the Bible. Many things could be included in such a Festival.

1. Displays of the work of children, youth and adults produced in their study of the Bible.

2. A speaker who is a translator or someone else who has special expertise and familiarity with the Bible.

3. A movie showing the history of the Bible or the work of the Bible Society.

4. Books for loan from church and/or public library.

5. A presentation by the minister about how he goes about preparing a sermon that focuses on a biblical subject.

6. Bibles, portions of Scripture and pamphlets from American Bible Society available for purchase or display.

7. Many mini-Bible study activities led by experienced persons for all age groups.

8. Dedication of Bibles for use in the sanctuary for worship or in classes for study.

9. Presentation of Bibles to third or fourth graders.

10. Mini-workshops to practice some basic Bible skills.

11. Launching a parish-wide program of increased Bible Study in church and homes.

12. A worship service that features use of the Bible in prayers, litanies, hymns, responsive readings and sermon.

The possibilities are almost unlimited. It takes only a little imagination and a lot of energy by some committed persons and such a Festival of the Bible can become a reality in your church.

64

Bibliography

Resource Books for Children and Youth

THE BIBLE AND YOU, A Scriptographic Booklet
Greenfield, Mass: Channing L. Bete Co., 1976
A sixteen page, illustrated, condensed overview of basic information about the Bible and its 66 books.

THE BIBLE IN BASIC ENGLISH
London: Cambridge University Press, 1965
A unique Bible in that it uses a basic vocabulary of 850 English words established by the Orthological Institute in London plus 150 words especially appropriate to the Bible.

Doss, Helen, YOUNG READERS BOOK OF BIBLE STORIES
Nashville: Abingdon Press, 1970
Many Bible persons and their surroundings are presented as being as real as today's heroes. Includes Bible references for each story.

GOOD NEWS BIBLE
New York: American Bible Society, 1976
A readable, reliable translation appropriate for older children, youth and adults. Contains: 1) introductions to each Bible Book, 2) Topical headings in each chapter, 3) Cross Reference Notes, 4) Word List, 5) Subject Index, 6) Chronology Chart, 7) Line Drawings and 8) Maps.

Henderson, Robert and Ian Gould LIFE IN BIBLE TIMES
New York: Rand McNally and Co., 1967
With a clear, simple text and very helpful illustrations this book provides an introduction for children of life and people in Bible times.

Jones, Mary Alice KNOW YOUR BIBLE
New York: Rand McNally and Co., 1967
This is a very good introduction to basic facts and features of the Bible regarding its origins and development. This would be most appropriate for fourth through eighth graders.

Maves, Paul B. and Mary Carolyn Maves LEARNING MORE ABOUT YOUR BIBLE and FINDING YOUR WAY THROUGH THE BIBLE
Nashville: Graded Press, 1972
Two self-instruction, programmed learning books designed for older children and youth. Some students respond enthusiastically to this approach of learning.

Northcott, Cecil BIBLE ENCYCLOPEDIA FOR CHILDREN
Philadelphia: Westminster Press, 1964

Northcott, Cecil PEOPLE OF THE BIBLE
Philadelphia: Westminster Press, 1967

But God's spirit entered me and raised me to my feet. (Ezekiel 3.24)

Both books are essential resources for use with children and youth. The text is very understandable, the illustrations are helpful, and the cost is reasonable.

THE RSV HANDY CONCORDANCE
Grand Rapids: Zondervan Publishing House, 1962
The only inexpensive, paperback concise concordance I know of for the RSV Bible. One feature I like very much is that under names of persons the references are listed biographically rather than in the chronology of the Bible books.

Tenney, Merrill C., ed. HANDY DICTIONARY OF THE BIBLE
Grand Rapids: Zondervan Publishing House, 1965
An inexpensive, brief but complete Bible Dictionary for youth and adults. Many, many scripture references for each subject. The primary negative feature is that the print is very small.

Terrien, Samuel GOLDEN BIBLE ATLAS
New York: Golden Press, 1964
In addition to excellent maps this book has a very helpful text accompanied by many colorful illustrations. This atlas is perhaps the best available for general use by children, youth and adults.

YOUNG READERS DICTIONARY OF THE BIBLE
Nashville: Abingdon, 1969
A very useful resource for children and youth with many key words defined, colorful illustrations, and Scripture references.

"He will go. . .and look for the lost sheep." (Matthew 18.13)

Resource Books for Youth, Adults and Teachers

Anderson, Bernard W. UNDERSTANDING THE OLD TESTAMENT, Third Edition.
Englewood Cliffs, N.J.: Prentice-Hall, Inc., 1975
In all three editions a standard work for all beginning, serious students of the Old Testament. The organization and clarity of the text make it a pleasure to read and understanding is increased by the use of many photographs, charts, and maps.

Barclay, William INTRODUCING THE BIBLE
Nashville: Abingdon Press 1972
A small book written by one of the best known and read Bible scholars in the world. Six chapters that truly introduce the Bible.

Beck, Madeline H. and Lamar Williamson Jr., MASTERING NEW TESTAMENT FACTS
Richmond: John Knox Press, 1973
Four volumes, each on different books of the New Testament. Designed for youth and adults. Programmed reading, art and activities, and tests are included in each volume.

Blair, Edward Payson ABINGDON BIBLE HANDBOOK
Nashville: Abingdon Press, 1975
Each book of the Bible is presented with a helpful outline and background information regarding the content of each book.

Brandt, Leslie F. PSALMS/NOW
St. Louis: Concordia Publishing House, 1973
A very meditative, contemporary, personal way of approaching the Psalms. Not a translation, not even a paraphrase but perhaps best described as a personalized transformation of the Psalms.

Frank, Harry Thomas DISCOVERING THE BIBLICAL WORLD
New York: Harper and Row 1975
A treasure of a book for youth and adults. Contains 255 photographs, 79 maps and an extensive text all focusing on the world of the Bible. The only negative feature is its cost—almost $20.00.

Furnish, Dorothy Jean EXPLORING THE BIBLE WITH CHILDREN and LIVING THE BIBLE WITH CHILDREN
Nashville: Abingdon Press, 1975 and Abingdon, 1979
Dr. Furnish presents an in-depth discussion on the focus, point of view and the how to of biblical instruction. Here is a challenge for invention and experimentation.

Gehman, Henry Snyder THE NEW WESTMINSTER DICTIONARY OF THE BIBLE
Philadelphia: The Westminster Press, 1969
One of the most helpful single-volume Bible Dictionaries for the lay person doing careful Bible study.

Hunter, Archibald M. INTRODUCING THE NEW TESTAMENT, Third Revised Edition.
Philadelphia: Westminster Press, 1972
A complete revision of an earlier work that has proven to be a very helpful resource to all serious students of the Bible whether they be lay persons or professional.

Johnson, James Weldon GOD'S TROMBONES: SEVEN NEGRO SERMONS IN VERSE
New York: The Viking Press, 1927
Included in the seven poems is one on Creation which is a marvelous, dramatic way to hear, feel and respond to the biblical message.

Kee, Howard Clark, Franklin W. Young and Karlfried Frohlich UNDERSTANDING THE NEW TESTAMENT, Third Edition
Englewood Cliffs, N.J.; Prentice-Hall, Inc., 1973
The Third Edition builds upon the excellence of the previous two editions. A very comprehensive, scholarly overview of the New Testament.

Laymon, Charles M., ed. INTERPRETER'S ONE-VOLUME COMMENTARY ON THE BIBLE
Nashville: Abingdon, 1971
A completely new 1,424 page commentary. Not an abridgement of the 12 vol. Interpreter's Bible. Seventy scholars contributed to the general articles and comments. Oriented to a broad readership of lay persons, students and ministers.

Look, a messenger is coming!
(Nahum 1.15)

Miller, Madelaine and J. Lane Miller HARPER'S BIBLE DICTIONARY
New York: Harper and Bros., 1954
One of the best, most readable one-volume Bible dictionaries for youth and adults.

Smith, Asbury THE TWELVE CHRIST CHOSE
New York: Harper and Brothers, 1958
A popularly written, easy to read overview of each of the twelve apostles.

Walton, Robert C. ed. A SOURCE BOOK OF THE BIBLE FOR TEACHERS
London: SCM Press, Ltd., 1970
A very comprehensive presentation of issues involved in teaching the Bible as well as extensive collection of articles on all aspects of the content of the Bible.

WESTMINSTER STUDY BIBLE, R.S.V.
New York: Wm. Collins Sons & Co., 1965
An excellent study Bible with General Articles, Introductory Articles, Numerous footnotes, cross references, and maps. Appropriate for youth and adults.

Other Griggs Educational Resources

INTO ALL THE WORLD

A resource for Adult Bible Study groups. Contains margin notes by the author, TRY THIS sections suggesting questions to consider and activities for the group to do, charts, maps, and special summary sections of main points. An outstanding resource for studying the New Testament.

TRANSLATING THE GOOD NEWS THROUGH TEACHING ACTIVITIES

Aids teachers to consider many creative ways to use the "built-in" resources of GOOD NEWS FOR MODERN MAN such as the Word List, Index, Line Drawings and Cross Reference Notes. In addition, there are many suggestions on ways of using Media such as slides, filmstrips, and cassette tapes for teaching the New Testament. Also included is a ten-page annotated bibliography.

GENERATIONS LEARNING TOGETHER

Don and Pat have gathered lesson plans and experiences they have had in teaching persons of several generations in one class. The book contains guidelines for leaders on "how to get started", suggestions for training of leaders, 40 session plans in series of 4 to 6 week units of study, and a bibliography of other available resources. Even though they have been designed for intergenerational groups, all of the session plans could be adapted to be used with classes of children, youth, or adults.

Bible Filmstrips from Griggs Educational Service (1731 Barcelona Street, Livermore, CA 94550)

One of the services Don and Pat Griggs have provided is the reissuing of out-of-print resources that should continue to be available for church teachers.

LIVING WITH JESUS (available Fall 1977)

A series of four filmstrips created by Annie Vallotton, creator of the line drawings for the GOOD NEWS BIBLE. Each filmstrip approximately forty frames with cassette narration and leader's guide.
1. Jesus and the Twelve Apostles
2. Jesus and Peter
3. Jesus as Teacher, Healer and Helper
4. The Last Week with Jesus

THE NEW TESTAMENT WORLD, 74 fr., color, cassette, leader's guide.

Geography of the New Testament Lands which will acquaint viewers with the Holy Land in a personal and visual way. Photographs and narration by Richard Rohrbaugh.

WHY WE CELEBRATE HOLY WEEK 56 fr., color, cassette, leader's guide.

One of the finest filmstrips available in the subject of Holy Week. Five sections each presented separately; Lent, Palm Sunday, Maundy Thursday, Good Friday, and Easter. Originally produced by UCC Press.

Bible Filmstrips from ROA's Films (1696 North Astor Street, Milwaukee, WI 53202)

The following sets of filmstrips are excellent resources to use for visual presentations of Bible subjects. They are only available in sets which are quite expensive. However, it may be possible to borrow one filmstrip at a time from a neighbor church or nearby media resource center.

Filmstrips that are helpful in Bible study include:

Abraham and Moses - eight filmstrips
Kings and Prophets - ten filmstrips
The Parables of the Kingdom - eight filmstrips
Paul and the Early Church - eight filmstrips

Cassette Tapes from American Bible Society (P.O. Box 5656 Grand Central Station, New York, N.Y. 10017)

GOOD NEWS BIBLE, New Testament, 15 cassette tapes
  Excellent recording, inexpensive.

GOOD NEWS BIBLE, Psalms, 2 cassette tapes
  No recordings available to match the quality and price of these from American Bible Society. New Testament and Psalms also come in combined package.

Cassette Tapes from Griggs Educational Service (1731 Barcelona Street, Livermore, CA 94550)

THE NEW TESTAMENT WORLD: Studies in New Testament Theology
  Fourteen 16-19 minute lectures by Richard Rohrbaugh coordinated with the book INTO ALL THE WORLD: An Overview of the New Testament.
  Lectures are:

Historical/Critical Study of the Bible
Old Testament and the New
A Study of Greek and Hebrew Thought
The Emerging Christian Community
Discipleship
Who is this Man?
What Really Happened: A Study
  in the Historical Jesus
Crucifixion
Resurrection
Parables of the Kingdom
Worship and Sacraments in
  the Early Church
The Meaning of Faith
Hope in the New Age

Cassette Tapes from Thesis Tapes (P.O. Box 11724, Pittsburgh, PA 15228)

Thesis Tapes has reprinted a series of fourteen programs produced originally by the United Church of Canada. Each tape includes four dramatic episodes focused on events or persons in the Bible. Each episode is approximately 15 minutes. These cassette tapes can be used in an almost unlimited number of creative ways.

1. PIONEERS OF THE FAITH: Introduction to the Bible, Abraham, Isaac, Jacob

2. STORY OF JOSEPH: The Brothers Plot, Pharaoh's Dream, The Silver Cup, Joseph's Family

3. STORIES OF CHRISTMAS: Isaiah's Prince of Peace, The Inn, The Shepherds, 900 AD looking Back.

4. MEANING OF CHRISTMAS: Hoped for Messiah, Angel's Announcement, Giving Gifts, Peter's Walk

5. JESUS — CHILDHOOD AND EARLY MINISTRY: Boyhood of Jesus, His Baptism, The Call of James and John

6. CALL OF DISCIPLES: Matthew, Storm in the Synagogue, Calling the Twelve, The Top Secret

7. THE EASTER STORY: Palm Sunday, Trial of Jesus, Crucifixion, Resurrection

8. AFTER THE RESURRECTION: Matthias is chosen, Peter and Lame Beggar, Stephen, Philip and the Ethiopian.

9. PAUL, PART ONE: Damascus Road, Paul's Escape, Barnabas, The Philippian Jailer.

10. PAUL, PART TWO: At Mars Hill, A Secret Plot, Shipwreck, In Rome

11. THE STORY OF MOSES: Son of Pharaoh's Daughter, Training to Be Free, In the Desert, Feast of Booths.

The Israelites were dancing and singing.
(2 Samuel 6.5)